Information and Knowledge System

Information and Knowledge System

Advances in Information Systems Set

coordinated by
Camille Rosenthal-Sabroux

Volume 2

Information and Knowledge System

Pierre-Emmanuel Arduin
Michel Grundstein
Camille Rosenthal-Sabroux

WILEY

First published 2015 in Great Britain and the United States by ISTE Ltd and John Wiley & Sons, Inc.

ISTE Ltd
27-37 St George's Road
London SW19 4EU
UK

www.iste.co.uk

John Wiley & Sons, Inc.
111 River Street
Hoboken, NJ 07030
USA

www.wiley.com

Library of Congress Control Number: 2015940032

British Library Cataloguing-in-Publication Data
A CIP record for this book is available from the British Library
ISBN 978-1-84821-752-2

Contents

Preface

Communication is an essential aspect of human life, and the opportunities provided by information and communications technologies are unprecedented. Information in various forms can now be transmitted across space and time. Paradoxically, to cite Feenberg [FEE 04], a distance has been created between individuals, of "disposable experiences, that can be turned on or off like water from a faucet". Individuals have thus become services, made available to others via a technical system, which can be activated or deactivated at will.

Originally, the computer was not intended as a means of communication. The Internet was not intended to serve as a conduit for this communication, and information technology was not intended for anything other than the automatic processing of information. Nevertheless, computers have become ubiquitous: information technology is everywhere, in our jobs, televisions, watches, telephones and even in our health. The quantities of information involved, unimaginable in previous decades, are now treated using concepts such as Big Data. Computers play an important role in our private lives, and our private lives themselves have become computerized; with data located at distant and unidentified points, they are in the clouds due to the use of techniques such as cloud computing.

Man thus makes use of all available tools to fulfill the essential need for communication. The use of information and communications technologies should not obscure the substance of these exchanges: information. Information which was previously passed from one person to another through human interaction is now exchanged via computer protocols, which aim to optimize systems interoperability without really considering human interaction; these interactions involve the exchange of much more than simple information. Information alone is simply a transcription, in the same way as a prehistoric painting on the wall of a cave, hieroglyphs on a papyrus or the neumes of Gregorian chant in a hymnal. Historians of today are constantly confronted with the challenges involved in interpreting this transcribed information (see Figure 1).

Figure 1. *Information can only become knowledge for you if it has a meaning for you. "King Ptolemy, the ever-living, beloved of Ptah, the god Epiphanes Eucharistos, most gracious lord": extract from the Rosetta Stone [FER 68, p. 43] (source: National Library of France)*

This book aims to highlight the advantages offered by information and communication technology (ICT) both in terms of information exchange and ensuring that the correct meaning is transmitted, allowing beneficial interpretation and the creation of knowledge. Information systems thus become information and knowledge systems. Although an information system may be based on ICT, it cannot be reduced to these technological aspects: users themselves play a role, acting as system components in their own right. These users process, store and transmit information, but this data has a meaning for them, something which does not occur in the case of technological artifacts.

Any attempt to limit information exchange to the framework of a digital information system using computer technology, to the exclusion of human contact, would most probably be seen as "totalitarian" within any organization [FEE 04, p. 180]. However, the number and availability of technological devices, the ease of use and the social character they may acquire all lead to more direct, frequent and essential interaction between individuals and the digital information system. Moving beyond the information transmitted within an organization, this book introduces the concept of information and knowledge system, which highlights the role of knowledge and the part played by individuals as holders of this knowledge. To do this, a clear distinction should be made between "information" and "knowledge"; moreover, it is crucial to be aware of the fact that information can have different meanings, leading to the creation of different knowledge for different individuals.

Pierre-Emmanuel ARDUIN,
Michel GRUNDSTEIN
and Camille ROSENTHAL-SABROUX
May 2015

Introduction

An evolution, either in technology or in its use, can have a significant impact on affected organizations. For Tran *et al.* [TRA 13], the ability to differentiate between evolutions which "will take root within organizations, leading to change" and those which "are more ephemeral, or have a much lower potential impact" is a key factor in ensuring the success of any Chief Information Officer (CIO). This monitoring activity aims to direct investment in relation to a situation and a context, but cannot be reduced to technological evolutions, as use and the evolution of use should also be taken into account.

Information and communication technology (ICT) seems to evolve independently of organizational activities. It forms an important part of our daily and private lives, sometimes even to a greater extent than in our professional lives. Any technological innovation may generate new uses; these new uses may raise new legal concerns, although this aspect will not be considered in detail in this book. Over 20 years ago, Chambat [CHA 94], discussing new information and communications technologies (NICT)[1], noted that technical offerings do not necessarily respond to social demands, but can generate new demands and new uses. Even further back, in 1974, discussing the contemporary use of "invented machines", Le Goff stated that:

> Men use the machines they invent while retaining the mentality they had before the invention of these machines [LEG 74].

1 No distinction will be made between ICT and NICT in this book.

Nowadays, in 2015, this remark is no longer truly relevant: the relationship between technological evolutions and changes in use has undergone a fundamental shift. While the use was formerly presented as a hindrance to technological development, due to inertia [GUI 93], it now continues to evolve faster than organizations are able to adapt to new technologies. Use evolves in the wake of technological evolutions, but in advance of organizational evolutions; it is essential to be aware of this fact when considering the processing, storage and diffusion of information in an organizational information system. Information systems are intrinsically linked to digital technologies, a consideration that will be discussed further in Chapter 2.

Web 2.0 is an example of a technological evolution going hand in hand with evolutions in use. The term "Web 2.0" appeared for the first time in 1999 when Palm Inc. was developing the first personal organizer with integrated web browsing capacity:

> The Web we know now, which loads into a browser window in essentially static screenfuls, is only an embryo of the Web to come. The first glimmerings of Web 2.0 are beginning to appear, and we are just starting to see how that embryo might develop. [...] The Web will be understood not as screenfuls of text and graphics but as a transport mechanism, the ether through which interactivity happens. [...] The hardware will be different from device to device; compare the interface of the Palm Pilot with that of the Game-Boy, for instance [DIN 99].

Web 2.0 is dynamic in nature and designed for use with multiple devices. It is a means of producing interaction, and has been labeled as "the social Web". This technological evolution led to changes in use; users are no longer content to simply consult Web pages in a browser (Figure I.1), but want to add their own content, whether from home, from their workplace or while traveling. This content is information, which may be processed, stored and diffused through a digital information system (DIS). It can also be a source of knowledge, when interpreted by individuals who are able to give a meaning to the content. However, this content cannot be considered as knowledge in its own right.

Figure I.1. *Internet home page of the Paris
Dauphine University in a) 1997 and b) 2014*

The domain of information systems will be discussed in Chapter 1.
Chapter 2 will introduce the domain of knowledge management, while
Chapter 3 is devoted to the information and knowledge system, using an
example taken from a real company. Finally, the book concludes with a
conclusion, offering perspectives for future developments.

Information Systems and Digital Technology

In this chapter, we will introduce the concept of information systems (IS), including a brief history of the domain. We will then define the concept of "digital" technology, and consider the role of IS and digital technology in a business context.

1.1. The concept of information systems

The concept of information systems (IS) includes two main aspects: first, the concrete organization which develops, innovates, communicates and records information, and second, the digital information system (DIS), an artificial, man-made object which makes use of the possibilities offered by information and communication technology (ICT) to acquire, process, store, transmit and render information in order to fulfill its role within the organization.

The key role of the DIS is thus to supply relevant information to each decision center, at all levels of the company hierarchy, for the purposes of monitoring, decision-making and innovation. In this way, the DIS is a crucial element in the decision-making process and in company operating and production processes; the DIS itself also interacts with these processes. The DIS is also a coordination tool. It plays an important role both at individual level, supplying information, i.e. representations used to solve problems in a decision-making process, and at collective level, transmitting shared representations throughout the organization.

According to Ermes-Groupe ESCP [ERM 94], "the information system of a company is the sub-system which contains all components of the company which interact through the provision of information. Its role is to provide information used to assist and monitor the operation of the business to all levels of the organization". The IS defined in this way is not an exclusively computerized system, as a distinction is made between the organizational IS, covering activity associated with the operation of the IS, and the DIS, which only concerns computerized content [NAN 92]. For Le Moigne [LEM 90], "information systems serve to represent, memorize and allow access to representations (in symbolic form) of the operating system for the decision system".

Definitions of some of the concepts used in this book will be given below. Systems science, also known as systemics, originated in the late 1970s. "Systemics is defined by a project rather than an object. Its roots lie mainly in systems theory, control theory and cybernetics" [NAN 92]. According to Le Moigne [LEM 77], the aim of systemics is "the modeling of complex perceived or conceived phenomena: the modeling of possible intentional interventions and their interconnected consequences for planning and forecasting purposes". IS have their origins in the systemic modeling of organizations, of which they form one of the three components. Further details may be found in publications by Le Moigne [LEM 74, LEM 77, LEM 90], Nanci et al. [NAN 92] and Mélèse [MÉL 79], among others.

According to Le Moigne [LEM 74], an IS is the system linking the operating and control systems. The operating system is the system in which physical or intellectual transformation takes place, and the control system is that in which decisions are made, in terms of aims and available resources. The IS enables decision makers and operators to access the information they need for, respectively, the purposes of control and action.

For Reix [REI 90], "the information system of an organization is made up of a set of methods and procedures for seeking, inserting, classifying, memorizing, processing and diffusing information. Its purpose is to supply this information in a directly useable form to different members of the company at the right moment, in order to facilitate correct operation and decision-making at various levels". Note that the processed information should provide assistance in decision-making, and sometimes in coordinating actions. The system needs to respond to requirements in terms of response time, relevance, accessibility, precision, cost and reliability of the information it provides. Information exchange occurs at different levels of command structures, and coordination issues may arise. Two types of coordination exist: "Vertical coordination, to avoid incoherency and conflict, and horizontal coordination, enabling users to work toward a shared objective, despite the division of labor. This coordination can either be carried out by mutual adjustment (direct information exchange) or by direct supervision" [REI 90].

For the purposes of this book, the following definition will be used, adapted from a definition given by the French *Commission Centrale des Marchés* (Central Contracts Commission, CCM [COM 90]):

> *An information system is a set of human, material and software resources, used by a user to carry out an activity within a given environment, which must be taken into account.*

An IS, as described above, is not necessarily computerized. The computerization of IS within organizations has led to a distinction being made between the organizational and technical aspects of these systems; the latter is referred to as the DIS. The difficulties encountered when designing a DIS lie in the separation of the two systems. The DIS forms part of the IS as a whole, and strong interactions exist between the two aspects. Churchman [CHU 71] established nine conditions used to define a system, which will be discussed below in the context of IS:

1) *An information system always has an aim,* that of providing necessary information to all levels in the management structure. How is this objective to be defined? How can necessary information be supplied to all levels? What is necessary information? These points are rarely specified in an IS, as analysts tend to focus on the solution to the problem rather than on the problem itself. In this book, we will attempt to follow the advice of Morin [MOR 77]), cited by Le Moigne [LEM 91], who stated that "we need to consider the system as a problem, rather than the system as a solution".

2) *The performance of an information system can be measured.* What is system performance, and how is this performance to be measured?

3) *An information system always needs to respond to the preferences of a user.* How are user preferences to be defined? What do these preferences mean? Which user is being considered? When identifying actors involved in an IS, the term "stakeholders" is generally used instead of considering individual users.

4) *An information system contains components which have their own objectives*. The objectives of information subsystems (components) are no easier to define than those of the IS itself.

5) *An information system operates in an environment*. The environment is rarely mentioned, and not often taken into account. Organizational aspects should be taken into account during system design.

6) *A digital information system must be paid for*. The buyers are rarely considered as stakeholders in the DIS design process, unless they also play a part in this process. It is important to give due consideration to the available resources when considering the functions to be fulfilled by a DIS.

7) *A Digital Information System has a designer*. The stakeholders involved in designing a DIS generally include an analyst (the designer) and a programmer. The way in which these parties relate to the final users of the system is rarely specified.

8) *The aim in designing a Digital Information System is to achieve user satisfaction*. How is user satisfaction to be evaluated?

9) *A Digital Information System provides a way of verifying the feasibility of the designer's intentions*. How are the intentions of the DIS designer to be verified, and at what stage in the design process does verification occur? What verification procedures are to be used?

A certain number of key questions need to be answered: Who are the stakeholders? How do they interact with each other? What is being done (i.e. what problem is being tackled)? How is this to be carried out (how is the problem to be solved)? Where (in what organization)? What influence will this place or context have on the system? What part does this context play in the user/machine relationship?

In all the cases, decisions are made based on the information. "The true role of the information system is in providing the simplest and most appropriate form of support to users when reconsidering raw data, redefining useful and relevant information, and rebuilding decision models in order to make them more effective" [COU 93]. Information is as important in diagnosing problems as in choosing appropriate solutions. All information is intimately linked to the subject of study, and is contextual. "An object should always be designed with an eye on the larger context: a chair in a room, a room in a house, a house in a neighborhood, and a neighborhood in a town plan" (Eero Saarinen, cited in [INM 93]). Information treated in this way needs to be represented. In designing a DIS, the representation of all relevant information is one of the main issues at play. A solid structure is, therefore, needed for the DIS design process, including defined stages, from information acquisition to transformation, representation, treatment and interpretation.

The rapid changes which have taken place in ICT in recent times have led to reconsideration of the way in which DIS are designed. This evolution can be described through four major steps, from the appearance of the first computers in the 1950s up to the explosion of ICT at the start of the new millennium.

1.2. History of the concept of information systems

Following a brief summary of the role and functions of a DIS, we will consider the main turning points in DIS design, triggered by technological developments.

1.2.1. *The centralized processing stage (1950s–1960s)*

This stage was characterized by constant, relatively stable linear development. The information technology (IT) developed during this period enabled tools to be designed to improve productivity in scientific and administrative tasks. Applications were implemented by large calculation centers. This method, known as batch treatment, was functional, specific and non-real time. The period was characterized by the use of mainframes, centralized architectures and work stations. DIS were centralized, and corresponded to "process-oriented" design methods, such as the Warnier method and the structured programming method. These methods were influenced by the technological resources available at the time, which were based on the use of files. They took a functional approach to organization and used a top-down methodology, consisting of a hierarchical breakdown of problems into subproblems, mirroring the image of the organization. The development cycle for systems of this type followed a strictly sequential cascade model.

1.2.2. *The data decentralization stage (1970s–1990s)*

This stage was characterized by a less deterministic, less predictable and increasingly complex evolution, marked by rapid change and increased competition. This is the period which saw the emergence of the microcomputer. The possibility of devolving some of the processing capacity allowed designers to establish non-real time handling processes for centralized data and/or real-time processes for decentralized data. Thus, DIS were called upon to handle large quantities of data, with key functions including memorization and calculation. These systems essentially handled "stable", structured data of types specified by the analyst and designer of the DIS [PRA 97]. The period was characterized by the use of databases and database management systems. The design methods corresponding to the appearance and expansion of databases included Merise and Axial, particularly in France. The development cycle for systems of this type continued to follow a cascade model, remaining essentially sequential, while establishing correlations with the results obtained at each stage of the development cycle (V and W cycles).

1.2.3. *The interoperability and standardization stage (1990s)*

During this period, organizations were focused on seeking new markets, creating a demand for new, powerful tools in order to establish communications between heterogeneous systems. Client-server technologies, object-based methods and reusable components led to the creation of conceptual tools and new, better techniques. DIS evolved from a focus on carrying out bulky calculations in non-real time to a focus on data storage, and then to an object-centered approach and finally onto enterprise resource planning (ERP).

Thus, over 70 object-based methods, or variants thereof, existed by the early 1990s. In 1997, the object management group (OMG) adopted unified modeling language (UML) as a standard [KET 98]. UML was the result of a broad consensus, taking account of the latest advances in modeling and software development techniques, based on the work carried out by experts in the field of object modeling. In order to standardize the DIS design process, the unified process (UP) standard was also submitted to the OMG. The development cycle described by this standard was iterative and incremental. At the same time, integrated management software packages began to appear, and were adopted by a number of businesses from 1996 onward. These packages aimed to offer a library of standard trade processes, adaptable using specific parameters, in order to automate the management of key activities. The packages provided a transversal view of businesses, unifying their DIS using a single format for management applications. Treating companies as a whole, using a tool to simplify the cycles involved in bringing products and services to market as far as possible, the "integrated packages" approach was seen as a reformulation of company applications, producing a more standardized form of DIS [LEQ 99]. Unfortunately, most of the companies did not apply the necessary organizational changes and trade processes when using these packages; this is a very real and widespread issue.

1.2.4. *The universality and globalization stage (2000 onward)*

A new form of "information economy" emerged in the early 2000s, based around the Internet and the increasingly global use of digital technology, creating the so-called "information highway". The universality of standards and the capacity for connection reduced blockages in information flows, enabling the acceleration of search, modification and transaction activities. The most striking visible results of these changes included the emergence of online shopping and the online marketplace.

Design methods have evolved over the years as new technologies have appeared, highlighting organizational dimensions: the connection between an organization and its DIS appears to be increasingly strong, and organizations are now "irrigated" by their DIS. The first stage in this process was marked by the predominance of computerized services. During the second and third stages, the roles and missions of those involved designing DIS evolved, and new actors became involved, in the form of project managers, representing the company in negotiations with contractors. This development required a shift toward collaborative working in order for application projects to succeed. The presence of project managers in the DIS design process highlighted the increasing influence of organizations on the design of their IT systems. Moreover, instead of simply managing, processing, recording and diffusing information, IT systems took on a role as "facilitators" in communication, explanation, coordination and cooperation activities. Moreover, the need for knowledge capitalization within organizations led to the development, proliferation and integration of certain technologies, partly as a result of research in the field of knowledge engineering. This created new capabilities in terms of knowledge management within organizations. The combination of these factors meant that a new approach to DIS design was required.

Based on these evolutions, the DIS development cycle came to be considered as an iterative, incremental and constructivist approach.

Stages	Development methods	Technologies	Development cycles	Actors in the development process	Design focus
1950–1970 Centralization of data	Warnier and structured methods	Mainframe and files	Cascade sequential	Computer scientists	Processing
1970–1990 Decentralization	Merise Axial	PC, SGBD and client/server	Cascade, V cycle, W cycle	Clients and computer scientists	Data
1990–2000 Interoperability and standardization	Object-based approaches: OMT, OOSE and UML UP	ERP and Internet	Incremental and iterative cycle	Contractors, clients, users, specialists and computer scientists	Organizationdata processing
2000 – present Universality and globalization	UML, RUP, MKSM, KADS, participative approaches and agile approaches	ERP, Internet and ICT Web 2.0	Incremental and iterative cycle, constructivist approach, agile method and rapid analysis design (RAD)	Contractors, clients, users, specialists, computer scientists, cognitics engineers, architects and urban developers	Organization collaborative working, knowledge management shared, diffusion information, sources of knowledge and workstations

Table 1.1. *The four stages of the development of digital information systems (DIS)*

The ubiquity of digital technology within businesses and its impact on the complexity of IS has resulted in a tendency to consider the digital aspect of these systems alone, i.e. a tendency to focus on the DIS. This reductive view of the IS is false. IT company specialists often make presumptions concerning the requirements of service employees, without taking account of certain specific trade factors. We will now consider the "digital" aspect of DIS.

1.3. What is "digital" technology?

The term "digital" was initially used, as an adjective, as the opposite of "analog". The *Concise Oxford English Dictionary* (2004) defines "digital" as "relating to or using signals or information represented as digits using discrete values of a physical quantity [...] involving or relating to the use of computer technology". The difference between analog and digital methods can be illustrated using the example of sound. Using an analog method, a vinyl disk creates vibrations in a diamond in order to generate an electrical signal, which is amplified to create a sound. Using digital means, compact disks (CDs) operate using a digitized sound signal, rendered discrete and reproduced in the form of numbers. This representation must then be decoded in order to generate a sound. In physics, an analog signal may include an infinite number of values between two points, unlike a digital signal.

Digitization is a basic process used in electronic technologies, involving the treatment of discrete numbers. Computers, for example, use base 2: series of 0 and 1. However, man was able to process numbers well before the appearance of computers in the second half of the 20th Century. Note that a computer is "an electronic device which is capable of receiving information (data) and performing a sequence of logical operations in accordance with a predetermined but variable set of procedural instructions (program) to produce a result in the form of information or signals", according to the Concise Oxford English Dictionary (2004). Thus, a slide rule, which is a machine for digital information processing, cannot be considered to be a computer as it is not electronic, unlike a calculator (see Figure 1.1).

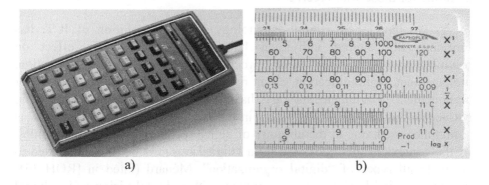

a)   b)

Figure 1.1. *A calculator a) is a computer, an electronic machine for the digital processing of information, unlike the slide rule b), which is not electronic*

In an organizational context, we consider that:

Digital technology is the set of artifacts which represent information in binary form, and which use Information and Communication Technology.

Digital technology has become increasingly mobile and ubiquitous. In organizations, digital technology is used at a range of levels, from the DIS used by employees to distribute information and share knowledge, to the smartphones used by individual members of staff, often key to their personal social lives. Digital technology can also be used by human resources to record clocking in and clocking out, for example, or for health purposes: the use of smartwatches means that health itself can be digitized, i.e. represented through a series of characters.

For certain Chief Information Officers (CIOs), digital technology is seen as being more for client-related, external purposes, whereas the IS is intended for internal management. However, digital technology does not always provide the type of automatic information processing desired. For example, certain organizations bring in external agencies to digitize their paper documents; once digitized, these documents become digital images which can be processed, stored and diffused using a DIS. This information can thus be processed automatically. Without optical character recognition (OCR), however, the processed information is not the content of the images, i.e. the text included in the paper documents, but rather the digital coding of the images alone. Computer science relates to the automatic processing of digitized information, independently of whether or not this information has meaning for those who receive it.

As we have seen, digital technology, via the evolution of ICT, has fundamentally altered individual habits, with a knock-on effect on organizational activities and processes, research and innovation, management, communication, client relations, logistics, skill sets and career management. Digital technology has also transformed the relationship between CIOs and the stakeholders in the IS. The term "digital business" is sometimes used, due to the ubiquity of digital technology within companies. In the context of this book, the term "digital business" will be extended to apply to all types of "digital organization". Ménard (cited in [ROH 14]) defines a digital business as "a company with a digital vision and a digital plan for all aspects of its business model". For Menard, this is "a global approach for the company, which wishes to create value via digital means, i.e. through personal and professional use of information technology". It is important to consider how the visions of IS, as presented above, and digital technology are to be integrated into company strategy.

1.4. Information systems and digital technology for business

The aim of an organization is to produce goods and services; a strategy and specific sets of skills are used in pursuit of these goals. Strategies are created using activities based around trade processes. These processes require information input. Consequently, from a systemic perspective, the "information system" is of the same nature as the organization in itself, and will always exist in some form. The DIS acts as a support for the IS. This is also true for family units, for example, which have an IS involving communications between members, with or without the use of ICT. Michel Serres draws an analogy with communication techniques used by American Indians, based on smoke signals. The fact that the IS and the organization are consubstantial is crucial; the IS itself is not visible, but is the way in which individuals communicate, whether face-to-face or using technological means.

DIS appear to have taken over, leading to a widespread belief that the IS is exclusively digital. Whatever the organization involved, ICT now forms a part of all processes. Technology has an impact on production processes, and these processes have an influence on technology: the two are interdependent. Over the course of their evolution, DIS have modified the way in which individuals communicate, as well as production processes, with a knock-on effect on business strategy. This strategy, used to determine the activities which take place, may both affect and benefit from ICT via the IS. These dimensions are all, therefore, interdependent, and the DIS is at the heart of their interactions.

An IS is made up of individuals, who communicate with each other directly and via the DIS. The IS supplies services to support activities and assist in decision-making. All entities and objects within an organization are now able to communicate, due to ICT, meaning that individuals can be considered as both components and users of the IS.

IS, therefore, involve a human and social dimension, characterized by the individuals involved, who contribute to the final processes used by the organization, and communicate between themselves. They also involve a technical aspect, in the form of the DIS, an artificial, man-made object.

IT offers features which can lead to uses different to those for which they were initially intended, leading to modifications at the organizational level, with changes to existing processes. A loop exists between use, design and technology. Discussions with CIOs have shown that technological evolutions precede reflection. Social networks are used constantly by individuals, leading to reflection within companies as to whether or not this should be authorized. Questions surrounding the way in which DIS are designed have not yet been fully answered, as no method yet exists to respond to the problem of organizational complexity. One emerging problem in the domain of IS, more precisely in terms of access to the DIS, relates to the critical issue of security. An IS supported by a DIS is integrated into a socio-technical environment, which itself acts as a support for all decision-making processes within an organization. These DIS offer new functions, leading to new usages and new behaviors, as we have seen with the emergence of smartphones, from both social and organizational perspectives. Processes are modified, creating new problems and new requirements. In this context, artificial intelligence, knowledge-based systems (KBS) and research carried out in relation to the decision process can offer solutions, although a single solution to all of these problems does not currently exist. The interactions between the possibilities offered by IS, technologies and organizations need to be reconsidered on a continuous basis by all those involved, in both private and professional contexts.

IS are transversal and apply to all services and disciplines, from financial management to human resources via accounting. The DIS supporting these systems are also transversal. A multi-disciplinary approach to teaching and research in the field of IS is, therefore, needed, and organizations need to recruit candidates with suitable training in this area. Clearly, technicians are required, but expertise in this area is also vital in other domains, including management, human resources, finance, etc., in order to fully understand the complexity of organizations and the way in which IS need to react. DIS are directly connected to users, who play a central role in the system, as well as to those who design, maintain and sell these systems. DIS are designed by human operators, for human operators: these final users may use the DIS in a way different from that envisaged by the designers.

The human dimension of IS can be obscured by the presence of digital technology. All participants in an organization are affected by the IS: management, the CIO, those responsible for DIS design, suppliers and, especially, the final users of the DIS. However, behind every DIS there is always a designer, and in front of every DIS there is always a user: these elements must always be taken into account, unless a fully automated robotic system is to be envisaged. This human dimension is essential, and user expectations need to be taken into account in the technological design process. It is also important to be aware that users may use the DIS in a different way than we might expect, as mentioned above.

IS involve communication, listening, personal implication, elements of psychology, mutual understanding and thorough comprehension of each other's requirements. A third dimension may, therefore, be added to IS model, in addition to organizational and technological aspects: this aspect concerns social and public responsibility, or ethics. The introduction of a new tool into an organization can have far-reaching consequences, something which may be referred to as digital ethics.

Given the ubiquity of digital technology and its impact on the complexity of IS, for each new project, the DIS design process needs to take account of the nature of information and the roles of individuals acting as components and users of the system. This consideration, combined with the results of research in knowledge management, has led to the creation of a tripartite classification of information types [GRU 01, GRU 03]:

– *main-stream information* concerns the flow of information concerning the state of production and operating systems in a company, notably those which are structured and recorded using databases, decision systems or ERP;

– *shared information* includes information processed by technological means which fulfill the following criteria:

- allowing instant transfer of digital multimedia documents including text, images, video and sound, and offering the possibility of asynchronous information exchange, changing our relation to time and space,

- enabling electronic conferencing, allowing users to effectively be in several places at the same time,

- leading to a transformation of working behaviors;

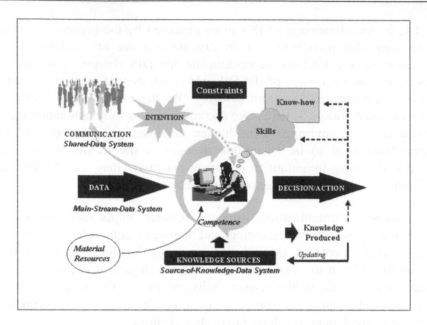

Figure 1.2. *Three types of information [GRU 03]*

These technologies mark a clear shift from earlier methods, due to the changing relationship of users to space and time, to the capacity for ubiquity which allows us to pass from the physical to the virtual world and from the manipulation of concrete objects to the manipulation of abstract objects. They generate real-time information exchange processes and knowledge sharing in a way not possible using older technology;

– *information as a source of knowledge* is notably the result of a knowledge engineering approach (KBS or expert systems (ES), analogy-based reasoning, etc.) which provides techniques and tools enabling us to acquire and represent knowledge. Knowledge is encapsulated in programs presenting this knowledge in the form of information which can be directly understood, accessed and handled by users. The data which a person receives, requested in relation to a specific context, are transformed by interactions with their own knowledge and skills: these data are activated in order to produce knowledge which is useful in understanding and solving problems, making decisions and acting.

The distinction between the three types of information is based on a definition of the term "knowledge" which does not dissociate the individual from the professional processes in which he/she is involved, the decisions he/she makes and the relationships he/she has with the surrounding system (individuals and artifacts).

It is, therefore, important to find the best possible means, in both technological and organizational terms, of designing a DIS in order to allow an actor at a workstation, carrying out attributed tasks, to share tacit knowledge and to access the information (used as a source of knowledge) required to understand and solve problems, make decisions, accomplish tasks and capitalize on the knowledge produced during these activities. Thus, designers must consider users as components of the system. They must also take account of the information which an individual, acting as a decision maker, needs to be able to access.

Knowledge management will be presented in Chapter 2.

1.5. Key points

The key ideas to remember from this chapter are:

– an IS is a set of human, material and software resources, used by a user to carry out an activity within a given environment, which must be taken into account;

– digital technology is the set of artifacts which represent information in binary form, and which use ICT.

2

Knowledge Management

In 1993, Peter Drucker stated that "increasingly, productivity of knowledge will be decisive in [the] economic and social success [of a country, industry or business]... In respect to knowledge, no company, no industry, no country has any 'natural' advantage or disadvantage. The only advantage it can possess is in respect to how much it obtains from universally available knowledge. The only thing that will increasingly matter in national as well as in international economics is management's performance in making knowledge productive" [DRU 93]. This vision has proved increasingly relevant over time. Companies have become aware of the value of non-material capital, particularly of knowledge capital [EDV 97, PIE 96]. Beyond the implicit approach to knowledge management (KM) on a daily basis, companies need to take a conscious and proactive approach in order to survive and to gain a durable competitive advantage [DAV 98]. Activities and processes should be put in place in order to promote optimal creation, identification and use of essential knowledge applied to their value-adding processes. This is the aim of KM.

In this chapter, following a brief historical overview, we will describe the two main approaches used in KM. Then, we will discuss management principles specific to the KM context. Finally, we will introduce the model for general knowledge management within the enterprise (MGKME). This idealized model is based on the key role played by individuals. It uses a managerial and sociotechnical approach to KM [COA 02] and attempts to combine the advantages of the two complementary approaches discussed previously.

2.1. Historical overview

The concept of KM first emerged in the early 1990s. In 1991, a "business knowledge capitalization" cycle was proposed, following on from work in developing knowledge-based systems [GRU 88], in the context of knowledge engineering, in which knowledge is considered as a collection of manageable objects. The concept of "knowledge capitalization" was defined as follows: capitalizing knowledge within a company involves considering the knowledge used and produced by a company as a set of resources, and drawing interest on these resources in order to increase the capital [GRU 95].

Other initiatives were being developed at the same time. The notion of knowledge assets was defined in 1990 by the initiative for managing knowledge assets (IMKA) project: knowledge assets are those assets that are primarily in the minds of a company's employees. They include design experience, engineering skills, financial analysis skills and competitive knowledge [IMK 90]. This definition laid the foundations for the concept of KM.

In 1991, Tom Stewart issued a warning to companies in an article in *Fortune* [STE 91], advising them to focus more on knowledge than on material assets: "Intellectual capital is becoming corporate America's most valuable asset and can be its sharpest competitive weapon. The challenge is to find what you have – and use it". In November 1992, Karl M. Wiig launched the first tutorials on KM, entitled *Knowledge Work in the Corporation: Knowledge Engineering for the Progressive Organization* during the third International Symposium of Knowledge Engineers in Washington, DC. In 1993, Peter Drucker [DRU 93] identified knowledge as the new basis for competition in a post-capitalist society: "More and more, the productivity of knowledge is going to become, for a country, an industry, or a company, the determining competitiveness factor. In the matter of knowledge, no country, no one industry, no one company has a "natural" advantage or disadvantage. The only advantage that it can ensure to itself is to be able to draw more from the knowledge available to all than others are able to do". In 1995, Nonaka and Takeuchi published a seminal work on knowledge creation and use in Japanese businesses: *The Knowledge-Creating Company* [NON 95]. In the English-speaking world, the concept of KM began to develop in 1994, and the concept took a more concrete form from 1996 onward, with the nomination of the first executives responsible for KM implementation. In the same year, Dorothy Leonard-Barton published a study on the role of knowledge in manufacturing companies: *Wellsprings of Knowledge* [LEO 95]. In 1997, we were fortunate enough to participate in the first seminar organized on the subject by B.P. Hall in San Francisco [HAL 97].

In 1997, "knowledge and intellectual asset management" positions were created in a number of companies, essentially in the English-speaking world [GRU 98]. In France, Cofinoga appointed a knowledge manager in early 1999, and Veritas included a KM function in its company organigram later the same year.

In 2000, Morey *et al.* published *Knowledge Management, Classic and Contemporary Works* [GRU 00]. This book was based on contributions from a large number of authors, and the theories and methods expressed in the work form the basis of contemporary KM.

A considerable amount of research has been carried out in the intervening years, applications have been implemented in a variety of businesses, and the domain of KM has been enriched by abundant written contributions, with the development of different schools of thought [ALA 01, REG 07].

Two different, complementary dominant approaches may be encountered: the first approach is said to be "technological", the second approach "managerial" and sociotechnical. A number of reference frameworks have been proposed, but very few give an equal weighting to the two approaches. Moreover, the technological approach, which tends to predominate, has often ignored the fundamental role played by individuals. Finally, the emergence and maturation of Web 2.0[1] created conditions for the convergence of these points of view, with the integration of sociotechnical aspects.

---

1 The expression Web 2.0 was coined by the author and editor Tim O'Reilly in 2004, while trying to find a title for a conference on the subject of the internet. In his web article [O'RE 05], O'Reilly proposes a series of possible applications, rather than a dogmatic definition.

2.2. Knowledge Management: two dominant approaches

Over the period from 1997 to 2004, the SIGECAD[2] group seminar organized 34 meetings with presentations and discussions on the emerging theme of KM and its interactions with information and decision assistance systems in companies.

This seven-year period saw the adoption of the term "Knowledge Management" by a wide range of individuals, each attributing a meaning to the term in accordance with their own personal perspectives.

More recently, the essential part played by information and communications technology (ICT) has become increasingly apparent, notably with relation to applications using Web 2.0. These technologies offer support for company activities and generate technical and organizational infrastructures, which can introduce an element of rigidity; they have also led to fundamental shifts in our relationships with space and time, knowledge, the perception of reality and the material world.

Guided by a study of interactions with information systems and decision aid activities, two broad, complementary approaches to KM may be defined as follows:

– *a technological approach* which responds to a need for ICT-based solutions. This approach focuses on coding explicit, stable and clearly-defined knowledge (generally of a scientific and/or technical nature). It concerns the implementation of computer-based tools, databases and specific techniques for knowledge acquisition and representation;

– *a managerial and sociotechnical approach* which integrates knowledge as assets for use in implementing the strategic vision of the company. This approach focuses on company performance, and on sharing and exchange of tacit, conjectural and dynamic knowledge (generally organizational knowledge). It involves decision processes, learning processes and skills

---

2 *Systèmes d'information, Gestion des connaissances, Aide à la decision* (Information Systems, Knowledge Management, Decision Assistance) are a series of seminars organized by researchers and practitioners working with search networks in information systems, knowledge management and decision assistance: Denis Bouyssou, Research director at the LAMSADE, University of Paris-Dauphine; Michel Grundstein, Engineering Consultant, associate researcher at the LAMSADE; and Camille Rosenthal-Sabroux, Professor at the University of Paris-Dauphine, LAMSADE.

management, networking and the use of social networks (notably communities of practice).

These approaches will be described in the next sections.

2.2.1. *The technological approach*

The technological approach is the most widespread approach to KM. Seen from the perspective of an information system, knowledge is implicitly treated as an object which is independent from the person who creates and uses it.

Although authors are generally careful to offer distinct definitions of the concepts of data, information and knowledge, the three concepts tend to be considered in terms of data processing in the context of IT-based applications. In this case, knowledge is simply a form of enriched data, as shown in the definitions included in the *Club Informatique des Grandes Entreprises Françaises* (CIGREF) report (Table 2.1), produced by a workgroup with the aim of specifying the aims and practices of major organizations in France [CIG 00].

Data	Fundamental and objective, qualitative or quantitative element, used as the basis for reasoning or for the implementation of processes.
Information	Set of unstructured data, organized to produce a message resulting from a given context, which is thus entirely subjective.
Knowledge	Knowledge is new information acquired via an intelligent process, study or practice.

Table 2.1. *Data, information and knowledge*

The examples of definitions given above show a desire for description, leading to a characterization and hierarchization of objects. With the Data to Information, and from information to Tacit and Explicit Knowledge (DITEK) model, Grundstein [GRU 12] proposed a way of describing the process by which data is transformed into information, and information into tacit or explicit knowledge.

The positivist paradigm underpinning the technological approach to KM leads to a hierarchical, object-based characterization and organization of knowledge. Authors who support this perspective are mainly interested in the contents of organizational knowledge, concentrating on the construction and management of knowledge assets. From this perspective, the technological approach results in KM projects which are carried out in exactly the same way as information system projects.

However, KM projects make use of specific techniques and tools which require particular skill sets. Thus, the distinction between the development of a KM project and that of an IS project only becomes apparent in relation to the technologies used. These include knowledge acquisition and representation techniques, e-learning tools, knowledge mapping, expertise localization, collaborative tools, automatic language processing, text-mining and data-mining, workflow, case-based reasoning and electronic document management, alongside navigation, search and visualization tools, the semantic web, Web 2.0, virtual reality environments and portals.

2.2.2. The managerial and sociotechnical approach to KM

The managerial and sociotechnical approach to KM takes account of the diversity of situations, the complexity of problems and the large numbers of different actors concerned by the KM process. This approach focuses on the connection between learning and action, and takes account of the constraints of the social system, giving meaning to time spent working.

This point of view is rooted in the theory of needs and motivations [OSB 64, MCG 71, DOR 99, PLA 00, COH 01], and particularly on a pyramid representation of the hierarchy of needs governing human behavior, proposed by the American psychologist Abraham Maslow (1900–1970). Maslow identified five levels of needs: physiological needs (food and water), safety needs (self-protection and protection), needs for love and belonging (being accepted and listened to), the need for esteem and prestige (to be recognized and valued), and the need for self-actualization (using and developing abilities, professional satisfaction). As Plane highlighted, "this contrasts with the ideas of Taylor, who only took account of the first two levels of need. Maslow identified needs and social motivations which have a deep impact on the world of work, such as identity, recognition, consideration and self-actualization" [PLA 00]. Thus, each employee must feel they belong to their company, and should be integrated into a network of individuals. They must have good relationships with others, and be respected and valued; they must also take pleasure from the accomplishment of their work. KM needs to provide the means to ensure autonomy and to enable employees to fulfill their own potential.

The managerial and sociotechnical approach to KM is concerned with activities and processes designed to increase the use and creation of knowledge within an organization, following two complementary aims:

– *asset creation*: essentially static, this involves the preservation, reuse and updation of knowledge. This aim raises a number of questions concerning the acquisition of tacit knowledge, alongside the modeling and formalization, conservation, access to, diffusion, evaluation and updating of this knowledge;

– *durable innovation*: more dynamic and concerned with organizational learning in the sense first defined by Argyris and Schön [ARG 96] in the early 1970s: the active creation of individual knowledge and its integration into an organization at collective level. This aim raises questions concerning the promotion and establishment of activities and processes to reinforce individual knowledge, and the "crystallization" of this knowledge at collective level through interaction, network-based working and experience-sharing.

2.3. Specific management principles for KM

A number of specific management principles used for KM and the elements involved in the application of these principles will be presented below. These principles are based on a managerial and sociotechnical approach, following the strategic orientation of the company. They lead to the adoption of a specific approach which differentiates the establishment of a KM project from that of an IT application project. In short, a KM project cannot be envisaged as the projection of a solution responding to a need. However, we must start by considering the problems generating these needs, and establish ways of accessing the knowledge required in order to solve these problems and to create new knowledge through action: to cite Argyris, we wish to access "actionable knowledge suitable for use by practitioners in daily life" [ARG 03, p. 15].

In the sociotechnical environment (i.e. the individuals and technical infrastructures making up the environment), operating processes and value-adding processes of a company are fundamental elements which underpin any vision of KM. These aspects represent the organizational context in which knowledge constitutes an essential performance factor.

In the following section, we will refine our definition of KM before turning our attention to the organizational context. We will then propose a vision for KM including guiding principles, *ad hoc* infrastructures, specific processes, and methods and tools.

2.3.1. *Definition of Knowledge Management*

The postulates set out in section 3.1.1 lead us to consider that knowledge is not a set of objects which can be treated independently of actions carried out by individuals. Consequently, rather than referring to KM in the same way as data or information management, it is better to speak of managing the activities and processes enabling the best use and creation of knowledge. This perspective was adopted in 2001 by the directing committee of the "knowledge capitalization and skill redeployment" project, led by the Exchange Coordination Research Industry (ECRIN) association, and used in the following definition of KM:

> *Management of activities and processes intended to amplify the use and creation of knowledge within an organization, following two main aims, which are strongly interlinked, underpinned by their economic, strategic, organizational, socio-cultural and technological dimensions: (1) asset creation, and (2) durable innovation.*

The asset-creation aim concerns the preservation, reuse and updating of knowledge, and is a static objective. The aim of durable innovation is more dynamic, and concerns organizational learning, i.e. the creation of individual knowledge and its crystallization at collective level.

2.3.2. *The organizational context*

2.3.2.1. *The sociotechnical environment*

The sociotechnical environment makes up the social fabric in which autonomous individuals from multiple cultures, supported by ICT and tangible resources, interact and converse using both physical and virtual spaces (the water-cooler, collaborative workspaces, blogs, wikis and communities of practice). However, the level of interaction is not sufficient, as highlighted by Stewart [STE 01]: "Making time to converse at every level of an organization is not an indulgence, not a luxury, it is an imperative". Stewart observed that the forms of interaction currently occurring leave no place for conversation: "Stories are not told and the associated sense of adventure is lost; knowing is not shared because questioning is not fostered; people become isolated, angry, resentful and do what they do with no real joy; while a business may be profitable, it is likely that it is not operating at anywhere near its potential".

2.3.2.2. *Value-adding processes*

Value-adding processes correspond to the value-adding activities described in Porter's chain of values [POR 85]. Porter identified nine value-adding activities, grouped into two main categories. The first category, "main activities", covers those which involve material creation and product sales, transportation to the client and after-sales service (internal logistics, operations, external logistics, marketing and sales, and services). The second category, "support activities", covers activities which enable the principle activities, and also provide mutual support (company infrastructures, HR management, technological development and supply).

Value-adding processes are elements of the organizational context in which knowledge is an essential factor for performance.

KM initiatives are developed within this context. As Tonchia and Tramontano   highlighted, "process Management, with the concepts of internal customers and process ownership, is becoming one of the most important competitive weapons for firms and can determine a strategic change in the way business is carried out". The authors specify that process management "consists in the rationalization of processes, the quest for efficiency-effectiveness, a sort of simplification clarification brought about by common-sense engineering" [TON 04]. Insofar as process management leads to structural changes when processes are re-engineered, KM activities need to be integrated in order to identify knowledge which is essential for these processes to reach their objectives in an efficient and effective manner.

2.3.3. The vision

Beyond material and financial assets, a company relies on the drive of its employees, the documents they handle (create, consult and update), and the ICT resources they use. KM is, first and foremost, a state of mind and a management style guided by this perspective.

Just as "at all levels, high-performance companies need to recognize the value and have a basic knowledge of the risks and constraints associated with IT in order to establish effective management techniques and establish adequate controls", (COBIT® 2000, Reference Framework pamphlet), this requirement also exists in the context of KM. While COBIT®[3] specifies that "promoting competition and cost efficiency implies ever-increasing trust in technologies, which thus become an essential strategic component in most companies", it is important to note that, in business, technology is not sufficient. It is unwise to ignore the role played by individuals, their interaction, knowledge sharing, creativity and ability to adapt, faced with an environment which is complex[4], hostile[5], uncertain[6] and unpredictable[7]. By analogy with the COBIT® definition, this has led to the establishment of a guide to the direction of KM, defined as "a structure of relationships and processes aimed to direct and control activities which improve the use and creation of knowledge, in order to consolidate the structure and processes of a company in order to reach objectives through generating value, while finding a good balance between the risks and advantages associated with good knowledge management" (see Figure 2.1).

The principles of KM governance provide a framework for KM to be aligned following corporate and IT strategies: when KM is centered on IT, the governance principles used are directly linked to IT governance

---

3 Guide concerning principles for the coordination and control of performance in internet technology (COBIT® 2000, 2002, 2005).

4 Consisting of many different and connected parts. Not easy to understand, complicated (*Concise Oxford English Dictionary* © OUP 2008).

5 Feeling or showing dislike or opposition (*Concise Oxford English Dictionary* © OUP 2008).

6 Not known, reliable, or definite. Not completely confident or sure (*Concise Oxford English Dictionary* © OUP 2008).

7 Not able to be predicted. Changeable or unreliable (*Concise Oxford English Dictionary* © OUP 2008).

principles, whereas when KM is centered on people and processes, the governance principles are directly linked to corporate governance principles.

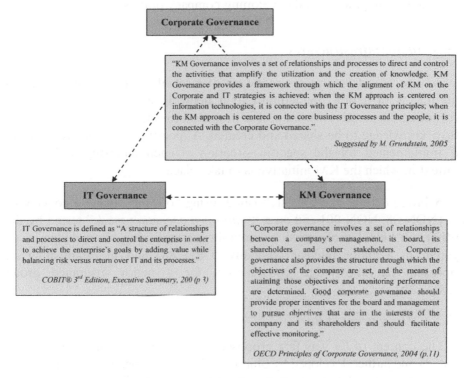

Figure 2.1. *Corporate governance, IT governance and KM governance (adapted from [GRU 12])*

2.3.4. *Guiding principles*

KM approaches follow two complementary and inseparable guiding principles:

– perfecting the quality and methods of access. These documents contain company knowledge, best practice and operating procedures, whatever the skill sets and functions involved. This provides the basis for a standardization approach, which can increase the productivity;

– promoting interactions between employees. These interactions lead to the creation of distinct competences, forming the added value of the company.

These guiding principles generally translate into three types of KM operations: creating a corporate, project or trade memory, creating communities of practice and developing company portals.

2.3.5. *Ad hoc infrastructures*

Ad hoc infrastructures are made up of a set of organizational resources and means of action. In addition to a network structure facilitating and promoting cooperative working, it is important to establish conditions which allow knowledge to be shared and created. A specific infrastructure needs to be implemented for the specific situation of each company and for the context in which the KM initiative is to take place.

A broad outline may be established, using both the Japanese concept of *Ba* [NON 98, NON 00] and on a *"semi-open operating mode"* tested by the authors on a number of occasions, notably in establishing a knowledge-based system in a major nuclear company [GRU 88] and in establishing an approach for knowledge conservation for a major insurance group [ARD 13b].

2.3.5.1. *The concept of Ba*

The concept of *Ba* was first proposed by the Japanese philosopher Kitaro Nishida and further developed by Shimizu [SHI 95]. To paraphrase Nonaka and Konno, this concept "may be seen as a shared space enabling the emergence of cooperative relationships between individuals" [NON 98]. This space may be physical (an office), virtual (a teleconference) or mental (shared experiences and ideas). It may take the form of a network of people with shared objectives, a place enabling the combination of rational reasoning with creative intuition via the creation of shared knowledge, or a platform for the advancement of individual and collective knowledge. The concept of *Ba* can take a wide variety of complex forms. As an analogy, the concept of *Ba* is similar to the *Plateau* device described by Christophe Midler in relation to the creation of the Renault Twingo [MID 93]. The *semi-open operating mode* used at the major nuclear company during the establishment of knowledge-based systems is, again, similar to *Ba*.

There are four types of *Ba*, which correspond to the socialization, externalization, combination, internalization (SECI) model of knowledge conversion proposed by Nonaka in a series of articles and books published in the early 1990s (Figure 2.2).

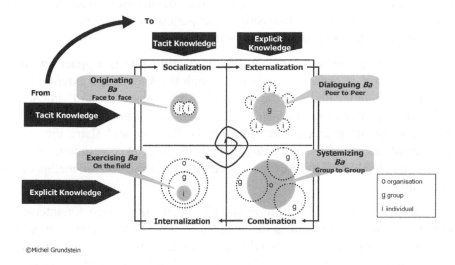

©Michel Grundstein

Figure 2.2. *SECI model and the concept of Ba (adapted from [NON 98, NON 00])*

For example, Nonaka and Takeuchi [NON 95] refer to the distinction established by Polanyi [POL 58] between tacit and explicit knowledge. Tacit knowledge is personal and context-specific, making it difficult to formalize and communicate; explicit knowledge, however, is codified and can be transmitted using formal and systematic language. The interaction resulting from the hypothesis that human knowledge is created and developed through social interaction between tacit and explicit knowledge is referred to as knowledge conversion. Thus, the SECI model includes two types of knowledge (tacit and explicit), a spiral-shaped knowledge conversion cycle (SECI) and three levels of social aggregation (individuals, groups and organizations). Each conversion mode is understood as a process of transcendence, i.e. one which crosses the limits of an individual, group or organization's own perspectives.

Nonaka, Toyama and Konno [NON 00] modified the names of the types of *Ba* defined by Nonaka and Konno [NON 98]. These four types of *Ba* will be described as following (Figure 2.3):

– the *Originating Ba* is a space in which individuals exchange feelings, emotions, experiences and mental representations. This is the "primordial" *Ba*, in which knowledge creation begins. The socialization phase develops in this space. Face-to-face discussion of experiences forms the key to the conversion and transfer of tacit knowledge;

– the *Dialoguing Ba* (formerly the Interacting Ba) is a space in which tacit knowledge is rendered explicit, through the knowledge externalization process. Through dialog, the mental representations and talents of individuals are converted into shared concepts and terms. This involves two processes operating in tandem: individuals discover and share the mental representations of others, and analyze their own mental representations at the same time. Dialog is the key to conversion, and the use of metaphors is essential;

– the *Systemizing Ba* (formerly the Cyber Ba) is a space for interaction within a virtual world, and is the location of knowledge combination. The combination of explicit knowledge operates more effectively in a collaborative environment using IT. The use of online networks, groupware, documents and databases is helpful in accelerating and facilitating the conversion process;

– the *Exercising Ba* is a space which facilitates the conversion of explicit knowledge into tacit knowledge, and is the location for knowledge internalization. Knowledge is internalized continuously through the application of formerly explicit and formalized knowledge in everyday life, or through simulated applications.

Participation in a *Ba* stimulates personal engagement, giving individuals the opportunity to move beyond their own limitations and perspectives. An awareness of the different characteristics of *Ba* can facilitate the establishment of favorable conditions for knowledge creation. The concept of *Ba* can also be used as inspiration for infrastructures including a durable knowledge-creation dynamic, via a tacit-to-explicit knowledge conversion cycle, with subsequent reconversion of this knowledge into tacit knowledge.

2.3.5.2. *The "semi-open operating mode"*

The "semi-open operating mode" aims to promote individual and collective learning and knowledge acquisition, and to encourage the emergence of new products and IT applications using the huge potential of new technological solutions. It attempts to reconcile the analytical approach specific to each skill set and discipline (insular and based on precise, detailed models) with the systemic approach (connective, based on global perception). It provides the conditions needed to establish a "field" of relationships which encourages interpersonal exchange and the creation of new knowledge.

In order to develop, the "semi-open operating mode" requires a multidisciplinary skills node and a space for development and progress, favoring contact and interactions between multiple cultures, in which actors are able to realize their full potential (Figure 2.3). This outline diagram, known as the semi-opened infrastructure model (SopIM), has been applied on a number of occasions, notably in the context of an experimentation, training and information center designed in preparation for the implementation of IT infrastructures at decentralized sites, and for a knowledge advancement and exchange circle associated with the implementation of knowledge-based systems.

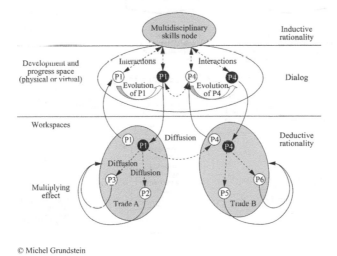

© Michel Grundstein

Figure 2.3. *Outline diagram of the "semi-opened infrastructure model" (SopIM)*

2.3.6. *Generic KM processes*

Generic KM processes respond to the need to capitalize on knowledge, defined as follows:

> *To capitalize on knowledge in a company, we must consider the knowledge used and produced by the company as a set of assets making up a capital, and drawing interest from these assets contributes to an increase in the value of the capital* [GRU 92].

Several problems exist, with which businesses have always been confronted. These problems constitute a whole which can be characterized by five elements and their interactions: identification, preservation, valorization, actualization and management. Each of these elements involves subprocesses intended to provide solutions to all the problems concerned (Figure 2.4). Thus, in addition to specific management principles corresponding to the management element of the issue, four generic processes may be identified which correspond to the solution of the four other categories of problems. These processes will be described below.

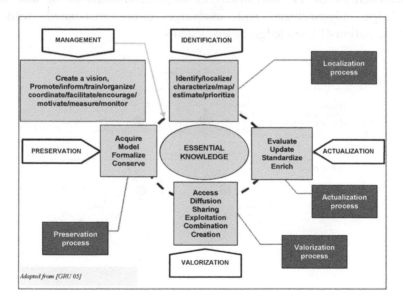

Figure 2.4. *Generic KM process and knowledge capitalization issues (adapted from [GRU 05])*

2.3.6.1. *Knowledge localization*

The knowledge localization process responds to the *identification* aspect of the problem. It concerns problems associated with finding essential knowledge, i.e. explicit and tacit knowledge required for decision-making and for essential processes at the heart of company activities. This knowledge needs to be identified, localized, characterized, mapped, estimated (in terms of economic value) and prioritized or ranked. This process aims to generate a feasibility study, leading to the proposal of an action plan. The study may be carried out in one of two ways. The first approach dissociates knowledge from action: this is an "audit" type approach, which aims to identify knowledge used and produced in an organization by studying existing documents and through interviews, following pre-established questionnaires based on reference models. The second approach, personified in GAMETH® [GRU 00, PAC 01, GRU 04, SAA 05] aims to connect knowledge with action. This approach focuses on operating processes and value-adding processes within a company.

2.3.6.2. *Knowledge preservation*

The knowledge preservation process responds to the *preservation* aspect of the problem. It concerns problems associated with the preservation of knowledge: when knowledge can be made explicit, it needs to be acquired from those who hold it, modeled, formalized and conserved. This is carried out using knowledge engineering activities [CHA 00]. When knowledge cannot be made explicit, "master–apprentice"-style knowledge transfer should be encouraged, along with interactions through communities of practice and other types of network.

This process is intended to memorize knowledge which can be made explicit, in the conditions described in section 3.1.4, and to establish conditions favorable to the preservation of tacit knowledge. These actions, laid out in the action plan, are small-scale undertakings. All of these efforts can only take on a permanent nature after evaluation in relation to improvements in the performances of the operational processes in question. These actions lead to the creation of a learning process, promoting improved understanding of problems and of the limits of selected solutions, often of a technical nature, without taking account of the organizational and sociotechnical dimensions of KM. On reaching maturity, these processes enable evaluation studies to be carried out, oriented by valorization processes.

2.3.6.3. *Knowledge valorization*

The knowledge valorization process responds to the *valorization* aspect of the problem. It concerns problems associated with the valorization of knowledge, i.e. using this knowledge for the development and expansion of a company, making it available in accordance with certain confidentiality and security rules, diffusing, sharing, exploiting and combining it and creating new knowledge. This process is strongly linked to innovation processes. It is based partly on *ad hoc* virtual or physical elements promoting interactions between individuals (concept of *Ba*, the "semi-open operating mode" or the plateau concept), and partly on ICT.

2.3.6.4. *Knowledge actualization*

The knowledge actualization process responds to the *actualization* aspect of the problem. It concerns problems associated with the actualization of knowledge, which must be evaluated, updated, standardized and enriched through the use of feedback, the creation of new knowledge and the acquisition of external knowledge. Issues of economic intelligence fall into this category.

2.3.6.5. *Organizational learning processes*

Organizational learning processes underpin all the generic processes described above. These processes are guided by specific management principles, corresponding to the *management* aspect of the problem. The aim of organizational learning is to increase knowledge and reinforce individual skills, while transforming them into collective skills via interaction, dialog, discussion, experience-sharing and observation. The key objective is to overcome defensive routines which hinder learning and change. Members of a company need to change their way of thinking, adopting constructive methods of reasoning rather than the defensive reasoning methods engendered by existing routines (Table 3.1).

2.3.7. *Methods and tools for KM*

The relevance of methods and tools can only be determined in relation to the context of a specific company and a specific KM initiative. Descriptions of most of the tools used in KM may be found in a number of publications [WEN 00, BAL 02, JEN 05] a response to KM requirements. This type of solution provides access to a collective (trade, project and company) "memory", and facilitates the creation of varied communities of practice. In this case, the functions of IT applications specific to KM are integrated into the digital information system (DIS). Moreover, techniques and methods taken from the field of knowledge engineering, artificial intelligence, computer supported cooperative work (CSCW), and the analysis and visualization of social networks are essential in order to give concrete form to certain elements, notably the sociotechnical approach, the establishment of "memories", support systems, and for the operation of communities of practice.

Global access to information through a company portal raises issues concerning the nature of information to which an actor or decision maker should have access (Chapter 1). From our perspective, an approach focused on individual knowledge requires the individual to be placed at the heart of the information system design process [ROS 96]. This process should not dissociate the user, a participant in the various entities making up a company (functions, trades, business units and projects), from the professional processes in which they are involved, the activities they carry out, the decisions they make, their relationships with others and their interactions with DISs.

Therefore, the portal should be envisaged as a collaborative information system, as described by Chua and Brennan in their study of collaborative knowledge management systems (CKMS): "A Collaborative Knowledge Management System (CKMS) is an integrated systems tool that enables collaboration between its users and its components" [CHU 04]. The authors note that "one of the most important components of CKMS is the knowledge workers, which are also the users of the system, and the workspaces they are associated with". Moreover, analyzing the ISO/IEC 9126 [ISO 91] quality standard, Chua and Brennan state that "existing interpretations of ISO 9116 account for their (knowledge workers') role as users however not for their role as systems components".

It is essential that individuals are integrated as components in the system from the beginning of the design process. As work by Tsuchiya [TSU 93] shows, knowledge depends on the mental model of the individual and on the context of their action. Consequently, knowledge resides principally in the minds and social interactions of individuals (see section 3.1.2). It cannot be considered as an object in the same way as a piece of data in a DIS. Similarly, information may be misunderstood as it takes on meaning via the interpretation system of the individual perceiving it. As mental modes and interpretation methods are mainly created by cultural factors, these factors are extremely important in cases where information and knowledge sharing form an essential factor in company performance.

The principles and management elements described above have been used in developing a model, known as MGKME. The MGKME, presented in the next section, offers a general perspective of what KM should be for an enterprise.

2.4. A model for general knowledge management within the enterprise (MGKME)

The MGKME is an empirical model which supports our definition of "Knowledge Management" (see section 2.3.1) and is based on three postulates (see section 3.1.1). It may be seen as a reference model to facilitate any business to evaluate the state of maturity of their KM system, and to refine their program of action in this domain. From a research perspective, the MGKME provides a framework for integration of the results of research in the KM domain. It leads to the use of design and implementation methods for KM systems in which the user is considered as a system component, responsible for the treatment and conversion of information into knowledge.

MGKME should be seen as an open model, to be used by all, with due consideration of the specificity of individual situations, to create a sociotechnical vision of KM, achieving a good balance between the technological and managerial/sociotechnical approaches. This model could provide the framework for the establishment of a KM direction guide, similar to COBIT®.

2.4.1. Description of the MGKME

The MGKME includes two types of elements: underlying elements (Level I) and operating elements (Level II).

The underlying elements include the sociotechnical environment❶ and the value-adding processes of the company❷. The operating elements include KM-specific management principles❸, actionable elements and *ad hoc* infrastructures❹, generic KM processes❺, organizational learning processes❻, and methods and tools used for support purposes❼ (Figure 2.5).

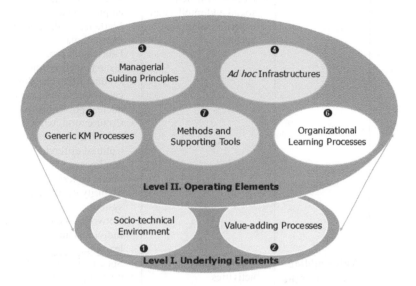

Figure 2.5. *The two categories of elements in the MGKME (adapted from [GRU 12])*

The component elements of the MGKME, the main resulting objects for analysis and the criteria used for characterization are described in Table 2.2.

Level of analysis	Elements of the MGKME	Main objects for analysis	Characterization criteria
Underlying elements (I)	Sociotechnical environment ❶	– Domain of activities of the company. – Relationships between technology, individuals, their roles, their culture, the tasks to accomplish, structures. Capacity for learning and innovation.	– Type of company. – Sector: finance, service, industry, administration, sales, building and transport. – Key element in the value chain: procurement, marketing, production, R&D and quality control. – Geographic distribution: local, national and international.

		– Degree to which social and intellectual capital is taken into account	– Size: small, medium (2,000 employees) and large. – Markets: local, national and international. – Fabrication procedures: discrete and continuous. – Product lifecycle: short (e.g. cell phones) and long (e.g. nuclear power plants). – Culture: oral, written, secret and technology-based. – Cultural differences between employees. – Social cohesion. – Maturity of information system. – Networks and communities. – Individual and collective learning.
	Value-adding processes of the company ❷	– Value-adding activities (main/supporting): Porter. – Operating processes. – Trade processes. – Design and development processes. – Innovation processes for products and services.	– Specific indicators for each type of process.
Operating elements (II)	**Management principles** ❸	– Vision. – KM direction. – KM-specific principles. – Guiding principles.	– PDCA cycle: Deming (1992). – Organizational level: Argyris and Schön. – Maturity level of KM. – Action plan in line with company strategy (factors for success, objectives, impacts on intellectual and social capital). – Identification and localization of essential knowledge. – Evaluation of risks linked to the loss of essential knowledge (vulnerability and impact). – Respect of quality, fiduciary and security obligations.

Operating elements (II)	**Actionable elements and** *ad hoc* **infrastructures** ❹	– Document management system. – Establishment of conditions favorable to interaction, communication and knowledge sharing.	– Entities concerned by KM: trades, businesses and transversal processes. – *Ba*, semi-open, or other type of approach. – Storage or flow policy. – Interactions. – Communication. – Sharing. – Adaptability.
	Generic KM processes ❺	– Identification process. – Preservation process. – Valorization process. – Actualization process.	– Suitable indicators based on those proposed by COBIT (2000 Reference Framework pamphlet): effectiveness, efficiency, confidentiality, integrity, availability, conformity and reliability.
	Organizational learning processes ❻	– Team-based learning. – Trials of new organizational apparatus. – Global vision and systemic approach to problems. – Routines (defensive and constructive). – Knowledge dissemination. – Movement toward change [ALT 00].	– Increased autonomy (critical thinking, distancing and self-mastery). – Good intelligence relationships. – Coherency between speech and action, theory and practice (shared interpretation methods). – Training and awareness (team-based learning). – Incentives (personal valorization and financial reward). – Disappearance of defensive routines/appearance of constructive routines. – Capitalization of experience.

	Supporting methods and tools ❼	– General tools and methods.
		– Results of semantic web and ontology searches (knowledge engineering and AI).
		– Multi-agent systems (CSCW – computer supported cooperative work).
		– Identification, visualization and analysis tools for informal social networks.
			– Internet technology.
			– Company portals.
			– Collaborative systems.
			– Analysis and visualization tools.
			– Semantic web.
			– Web 2.0: Blogs, Podcasts, Instant Messaging, RSS, Wikis (Social Network tools).
			– Content management systems.
			– Electronic document management.
			– Data warehouses.
			For each method and tool:
			  - Cost.
			  - Relevance.
			  - ROI.

Table 2.2. *Component elements of the MGKME*

2.4.2. *State indicators for knowledge management systems*

State indicators for KM systems facilitate companies to identify their position in relation to the reference model (MGKME). The components of an enterprise's KM system constitute a partial or total realization of the elements of the MGKME (Figure 2.6).

This approach is derived from the maturity model defined by the Software Engineering Institute to measure the maturity of a software development function. Table 2.3 gives descriptions of maturity levels adapted from the COBIT (COBIT® 2000, Management guide pamphlet, reference framework) and are applicable when analyzing any component of the MGKME.

Enterprise's KMS is the partial or total implementation of MGKME's elements.

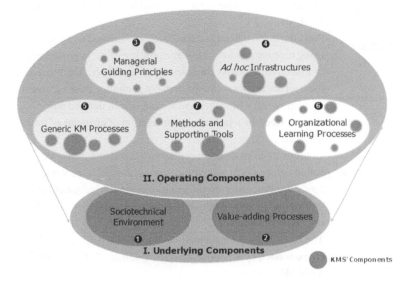

Figure 2.6. *Components of an enterprise's knowledge management system (from [GRU 08])*

Maturity level	Characteristics
Level 0 Non-existent	Total absence of an identifiable Knowledge Management system. The company is not aware that Knowledge Management should be studied and taken into consideration.
Level 1 Initial/*Ad hoc*	The company is aware of the importance of Knowledge Management, but does not have a global vision. There is no standardized process, but approaches tend to be made individually or on a case-by-case basis. Establishment of a Knowledge Management system or any of its components has not been organized.
Level 2 Repeatable but intuitive	The Knowledge Management system is poorly defined and characterized by a partial implementation of elements of the MGKME. Processes have been developed to the point where different individuals carrying out the same task to use similar procedures. There is no formal training or communication concerning standard processes, and responsibility is left to individuals. There is a strong reliance on individual knowledge, increasing the probability of errors.

Level 3 Defined Process	The Knowledge Management system is well defined and characterized by a partial implementation of elements of the MGKME. Procedures have been standardized, documented and communicated using training sessions. However, the use of these procedures is left to individual initiative, and deviations are likely. The procedures themselves are not sophisticated, but formalize existing practices.
Level 4 Managed and Measurable	The Knowledge Management system is well defined and characterized by a partial implementation of elements of the MGKME. Conformity to procedures can be monitored and measured, and action can be taken when processes appear not to be working correctly. Processes are subject to constant improvement and correspond to good practice. Automization and tool use is limited or only partially applied.
Level 5 Optimized	The Knowledge Management system is well defined and characterized by an optimal implementation of all elements of the MGKME. Processes have attained the level of best practice, following constant improvements and comparisons with other companies.

Table 2.3. *KM maturity levels*

The Appendix gives a definition of seven "golden rules" for the successful implementation of a KM project.

2.5. Conclusions

The fundamental notions presented in this chapter are derived from our experience and research activities. They are intended to provide a platform for reflection, giving individuals the liberty to make their own choices for specific situations and in connection with their own values.

In any company using ICT, components exist which give concrete form to elements of the MGKME, at least partially, whether or not this model is explicitly recognized. Thus, the Knowledge Management System (KMS) of a company may be more or less developed depending on its state of maturity. The KMS may be as simple as one or more local computer applications, established in departments and/or operating units within the company. It may take a more general form, following company strategy, taking account of a specific approach and of specific management principles, based on a number of elements: a sociotechnical approach, knowledge engineering methods and AI techniques, CSCW, tools for the implementation of ICT, notably Web 2.0, and/or a collective learning network enabling continuous improvement of individual and collective skills.

However, when KM becomes a more formal priority for a company, with the creation of a KMS project, existing components must be integrated into a general vision. Thus, the MGKME becomes a point of reference in evaluating the true state of the existing KMS, including its maturity level (see section 2.4.2), in order to propose directions for work and a program of actions intended to launch new initiatives which will, in time, result in the realization of all elements of the MGKME. From our perspective, this framework is vital for the initiation and development of KM initiatives.

Our research work and practical experience in KM and our teaching activities in relation to information systems, digital development and the importance of knowledge in organizations have lead us to introduce a new concept, that of the enterprise's information and knowledge systems (EIKS).

2.6. Key points

The key ideas to remember from this chapter are:

– KM is the management of activities and processes intended to amplify the use and creation of knowledge within an organization, following two main aims, which are strongly interlinked, underpinned by their economic, strategic, organizational, sociocultural and technological dimensions: (1) asset creation, and (2) durable innovation;

– there are two approaches to KM: the technological approach and the managerial and sociotechnical approach.

The Enterprise's Information and Knowledge System (EIKS)

We will begin this chapter by introducing basic theories before presenting the enterprise's information and knowledge system (EIKS). The difference between knowledge system (KS) and knowledge-based systems will then be explained. The evolution of the EIKS will be discussed, and a representative example of an EIKS encountered in a business situation will then be presented.

3.1. Basic theories

The enterprise's information and knowledge system (EIKS) draws inspiration from research work and practical experience in the domains of information systems (see Chapter 1) and knowledge management (see Chapter 2), which are founded on the basic theories presented in this section.

3.1.1. *Three fundamental postulates*

Our suggested approach to knowledge management is based on three postulates and one definition, resulting from our experience and research.

Postulate 1: Knowledge is not an object

This postulate is based on the theories of Tsuchiya [TSU 93]. Knowledge is not an object, but results from the encounter between data and a subject, and takes root in the memory of an individual via their own interpretation system. In other words, we consider that knowledge only exists as the result of the meeting between a subject and data. This individual knowledge is tacit, and it may or may not be possible to make it explicit. It may undergo later transformation into collective knowledge if it is shared with other people.

This postulate leads us to consider that any item of knowledge rendered explicit and codified in a digital application, in fact, implies information, which will take on meaning for a person in relation to their context, situation and the activation of one or more interpretative frameworks. This is known as "information which is a source of knowledge for someone".

Postulate 2: Knowledge is linked to action

From a company perspective, knowledge is linked to action and is essential for its accomplishment. Knowledge is finalized by action. This perspective is based on a definition of knowledge which does not dissociate the person at the heart of company processes from their actions, decisions and relationships with the surrounding system (people and artifacts). This leads to a focus on the knowledge linked to the activities of actors/decision makers, engaged in the finalized processes of the company – support processes and value-adding processes [POR 85].

Postulate 3: A company's knowledge includes two main categories of knowledge

Knowledge in a company can be classified into two broad categories: first, explicit knowledge, including all tangible elements, and second, tacit knowledge [POL 66], including all intangible elements (skills). It may or may not be possible to articulate tacit knowledge in such a way that it becomes explicit, i.e. made explicit by someone. Tangible elements are collective knowledge and take the form of knowledge which is formalized and codified using physical supports (databases, procedures, plans, models, algorithms, analysis and summary documents) or is encapsulated in management systems, production systems or products. Intangible elements are embodied by the people who, collectively, possess them in the form of "routines" – individual and collective unwritten rationales for action [NEL 82] – or by individuals in the form of knowledge of the history or context of decisions and environmental knowledge (clients, competitors, technologies, socioeconomic influence factors, etc.). This dichotomy is illustrated in Table 3.1, which also differentiates between knowledge of an individual or collective nature.

Company knowledge (explicit knowledge)	Company skills (tacit knowledge embodied by individuals)	
Collective knowledge *apparently objectivized knowledge*	**Collective knowledge** *routines*	**Personal knowledge** *private knowledge*
Formalized in documents and/or coded in software	Knowledge incorporated into regular and predictable behavioral models	Abilities, knacks, "trade secrets", knowledge of history and contexts of decisions, of environment (clients, competitors, technologies), factors of socioeconomic influence
Knowledge-source information	***Defensive routines*** →obstacles to change ***Constructive routines*** →promote innovation and change	***Specific, individual knowledge*** →volatile knowledge, dependent on the presence of a specific person

Table 3.1. *The two categories of knowledge in a company*

3.1.2. *Creation of individual and tacit knowledge*

The concepts of "sense-reading" and "sense-giving"

Our approach is based on the theories of Tsuchiya [TSU 93] concerning the creation of "organizational knowledge". Using the concepts of "sense-giving" and "sense-reading" studied by Polanyi [POL 67], Tsuchiya observed that while the terms "data", "information" and "knowledge" are often used interchangeably, a clear distinction exists between the three: "Although the terms 'datum', 'information', and 'knowledge' are often used interchangeably, there exists a clear distinction among them. When datum is sense-given through interpretative framework, it becomes information, and when information is sense-read through interpretative framework, it becomes knowledge" [TSU 93]. The diagram presented in Figure 3.1 shows our own representation of this perspective: the tacit knowledge residing in our brains is the result of the sense that we give, via our interpretation mechanisms, to data which we perceive among the information transmitted to us.

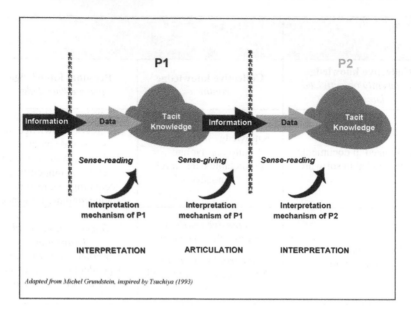

Figure 3.1. *Creation of individual tacit knowledge*

The sense-giving and sense-reading processes are defined by Polanyi [POL 67] as follows: "Both the way we endow our own utterance with meaning and our attribution of meaning to the utterances of others are acts of tacit knowing. They represent sense-giving and sense-reading within the structure of tacit knowing". Tsuchiya [TSU 93] added the concept of interpretative frameworks, which, from our perspective, may be considered as a mental model, as defined by Jones *et al.* [JON 11]: "Mental models are personal, internal representations of external reality that people use to interact with the world around them. They are constructed by individuals based on their unique life experiences, perceptions, and understandings of world. Mental models are used to reason and make decisions and can be the basis of individual behaviors. They provide the mechanism through which new information is filtered and stored".

We continually interpret information in the course of sense-reading processes. In an organization, information may be transmitted through speaking, writing, acting or more generally via an information system (IS). Knowledge may be:

– *explicit*: this knowledge is a social construct, and may be supported by information and communication technology (ICT). Individuals, as well as computers, are "information-processing systems", as stated by Hornung [HOR 09];

– *tacit*: this knowledge may not always be structured, notably, as Polanyi [POL 58] states, as "we know more than we can say".

The term "explicit knowledge" refers to explicitly-rendered knowledge: this is tacit knowledge which is rendered explicit by an individual, and becomes information which is a source of knowledge for another person. It is, essentially, that which we know and can express verbally, in response to Polanyi [POL 58], cited above. The term "explicit knowledge" is often used, notably by Nonaka and Konno [NON 98] and Nonaka and Takeuchi [NON 95], but this does not fully reflect the dynamic process where tacit knowledge is rendered explicit by an individual. Every item of information, i.e. knowledge which has been rendered explicit, can be seen as an individual cognitive construct produced within a highly specific context in an organization.

Wiig [WII 04], who highlights the discontinuity between information and knowledge, describes this process clearly in a different way: "The process, by which we develop new knowledge, uses prior knowledge to make sense of the new information and, once accepted for inclusion, internalizes the new insights by linking with prior knowledge. Hence, the new knowledge is as much a function of prior knowledge as it is of received inputs. A discontinuity is thus created between the received information inputs and the resulting new knowledge" [WII 04].

Consequently, we see that knowledge is not an object independent of an actor. Thus, formalized and codified knowledge which is independent of individuals may only be considered to be information, that we call "information which is a source of knowledge for someone". Moreover, as Haeckel [HAE 00] states, we need to distinguish between "the knowledge of knower and the codification of that knowledge".

3.1.3. *Commensurability of interpretative frameworks*

Tsuchiya highlights the way in which organizational knowledge is created through dialog. For organizational knowledge to be created, essential for decision-making and action purposes, the interpretative frameworks of each member of the organization must include a certain level of shared representations, known as "commensurability". For Tsuchiya, "it is important to clearly distinguish between sharing information and sharing knowledge. Information becomes knowledge only when it is sense-read through the interpretative framework of the receiver. Any information inconsistent with his interpretative framework is not perceived in most cases. Therefore, commensurability of interpretative frameworks of members is indispensable for individual knowledge to be shared" [TSU 93].

Thus, information can only be assimilated to knowledge when there is a high level of commensurability between the interpretative frameworks of individuals, allowing them to interpret information in the same manner and to give it the same meaning. This is "information as a source of knowledge for someone".

In these cases, formalized and codified knowledge takes on the same meaning for each individual. This allows us to speak of knowledge bases and knowledge flows. However, we must take account of the fact that interpretative frameworks evolve and are not rigid thought structures, notably due to evolutions in contexts and situations. Thus, scientific progress, innovation and the creation of new techniques and methods, the influence of generations brought up with the Internet, the impact of identity crises and multiculturalism, all modify individual interpretation mechanisms and create ruptures in commensurability. The concept of commensurability of interpretative frameworks has notably been studied by Arduin [ARD 13a] with the aim of creating a system of measurement.

3.1.4. *Conditions in which knowledge can be assimilated to an object*

The previous sections may be summarized by stating that knowledge is not an object but the result of an interaction between a person and an item of data. This individual knowledge is tacit, and it may or may not be possible to express it. This knowledge becomes collective when it is shared with others, and if the interpretative frameworks of these others are "commensurable", i.e. allow a minimum level of shared interpretation of meaning, shared between all members of the organization. This idea is in apparent opposition to the idea of objectifiable knowledge, used in knowledge engineering, in the context of techniques and methods for the acquisition and representation of knowledge. However, for applications within this field of research, where knowledge is implemented in the form of computer systems, these realizations may be seen as coded projections of acquired, formalized and represented knowledge. These projections, which are naturally simplifications, thus only constitute "information as a source of knowledge" for the person or artifact able to interpret them.

Moreover, it is paradoxical to think that knowledge is not objectifiable, if we consider technical knowledge (descriptive, normative or prescriptive knowledge applied to material or immaterial objects) or scientific knowledge, which has a value of absolute truth and is, by nature, universal. This knowledge is often confused with the media used for its diffusion. This media, in the form of material or electronic documents, only truly contains "information as a source of knowledge" for populations able to interpret it in accordance with their profession, field of research or interest, beliefs and culture.

The concept of "commensurability" allows us to move beyond this paradox. For example, we may consider that, when a significant degree of commensurability between interpretative frameworks is present, the knowledge transmitted through documents or other media is apparently objective, i.e. independent of the person interpreting it. This is notably the case for industrial knowledge, in cases where asset-based capitalization targets a population of specialists from certain specific knowledge fields. In these cases, knowledge might be managed as "knowledge objects". This idea is used in solutions such as document management systems (DMS), company memory bases and/or project memory bases. However, it is important to remember that which is formalized, whatever form it takes, can only ever be information, which only takes on meaning for individuals with shared interpretative frameworks. Interpretative frameworks evolve as populations of actors change, which can lead to difficulties of access, interpretation and to the risk of erroneous use of these "knowledge objects".

In conclusion, knowledge may be assimilated to an object, and can consequently be managed in the same way as information under a certain number of conditions: the knowledge has been rendered explicit and codified, is stable and well-defined, and is recognized by a given specific homogeneous population. Based on this idea, our research work and practical experience have led us to introduce the EIKS.

3.2. The enterprise's information and knowledge system

The EIKS is built on a socio-technical fabric (individuals in interaction with each other, with machines and with the system itself). It is made of (Figure 3.2):

– an *Information System*, made up of individuals, who process information, to which they give meaning in a given context. This information may be transmitted, memorized, processed and diffused by the individuals themselves or by the digital information system (DIS);

– a *Knowledge System* (KS), made up of both tacit knowledge embodied by individuals and explicit knowledge which has been formalized and codified using supports of various forms, digital or otherwise (documents, videos, photos, etc.). Under certain conditions (see section 3.1.4), knowledge which has been rendered explicit and codified in this way may be transmitted, memorized, processed and diffused by the DIS. It may be assimilated to information, and referred to as "information as a source of knowledge for someone";

– a *Digital Information System*, an artifact constructed using ICT.

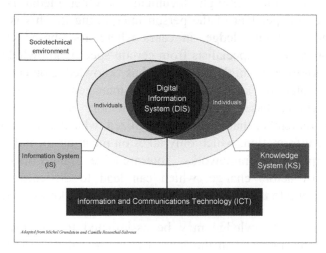

Figure 3.2. *The enterprise's information and knowledge system (EIKS)*

Thus, rather than knowledge, the IS carries *information as a source of knowledge*. Only individuals can possess genuine knowledge, resulting from their interpretation of information [TSU 93], so that:

> *The individual is a carrier of knowledge and a processor of information, and is a component of the Enterprise's Information and Knowledge System.*

By formalizing and codifying information which has been rendered explicit in an IS, we create information which will be a source of knowledge for others. The author of this information possesses knowledge, which he/she formalizes, giving meaning to the information he/she creates. This information will be a source of knowledge for individuals who "read" the same meaning. This process is, therefore, not simply an exchange of information, but involves the transfer of knowledge, in the sense used by Davenport and Prusak [DAV 98]. Figure 3.3 shows a unified modeling language (UML) representation of the EIKS.

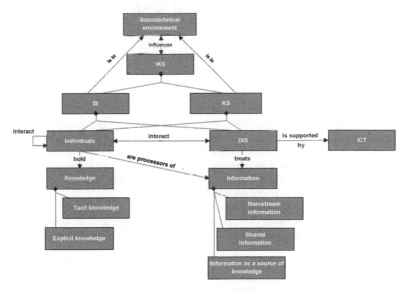

Figure 3.3. *UML representation of the Enterprise's Information and Knowledge System (EIKS)*

Note, once again, that the individual is both a user and a component of the system. This is supported by Chua and Brennan's study of collaborative knowledge management systems (CKMS) [CHU 04] mentioned in section 2.1.7. Referring to our postulates, we believe that knowledge resides in individual minds and their social interactions.

3.3. A knowledge system is not a knowledge-based system

A KS is not a knowledge-*based* system. Since the appearance of MYCIN, one of the first knowledge-based systems, in the early 1970s, mass computerization in business has clearly demonstrated the limits of these technological systems: knowledge is treated as an object, to which inference rules may be applied using artificial intelligence (AI) tools. Thus, a computer may "think" using the "knowledge" which it "possesses". In reality, an algorithm is used to connect input to output, based on static variables stored in the memory. MYCIN, for example, allowed the identification of bacteria responsible for serious infections, and recommended the correct antibiotics and doses. Figure 3.4 shows the MYCIN interface in 1974. This knowledge-based system used user-machine dialog to refine results as a function of data input. The possible responses were coded in advance, alongside inference rules and a certain amount of basic data.

*****Welcome from MYCIN*****

Instructions?: (Yes or No)
**YES
    I am a computer program named MYCIN that has been designed to advise you regarding an appropriate choice of infectious disease therapy. I understand that you have a patient from whom a possibly positive culture (called CULTURE-1) has been obtained. Please answer the following questions, terminating each response with RETURN.
    If you are not certain of your answer, you may modify the response by inserting a certainty factor (a number from 1 to 10) in parentheses after your response. Absolute certainty (10) is assumed for every unmodified answer.
    If you wish to change an answer to a previous question, enter CHANGE followed by the number(s) of the question(s) to be altered. Try to avoid going back, however, because the process requires reconsidering the patient from the beginning and it may therefore be slow.
    Note that you may also enter UNK (for UNKnown) if you do not know the answer to a question, ? if you would like to see some examples of recognized responses, ?? if you want to see all recognized responses, the word RULE if you would like to see the decision rule which has generated the question being asked, the word WHY if you would like to see a more detailed explanation of the question, or the letters QA if you would like to interrupt the consultation in order to ask questions regarding the current status of the program's reasoning. If you are ever puzzled about what options are available to you during a consulation, enter the word HELP and a list of options will be listed for you.

Figure 3.4. *The MYCIN interface in 1974 [SHO 76]*

In MYCIN, the human operator is considered as an additional processor, or as a partner [ROS 96], inserting input data and processing the displayed output data. Our interactions with the world around us mean that we are members of an IS, within which we process, store and transmit information. MYCIN is an example of a knowledge-*based* system, a computer program using AI tools to infer results based on (1) data stored in the memory, (2) inference rules and (3) data input from a user.

Restricted to laboratory settings in the 1970s, knowledge-based systems began to be used in enterprises during the 1980s, with the appearance of "expert systems". These systems were intended to simulate the decision capacities of human experts [JAC 98]. A wide range of knowledge capitalization (not capitalization *on* knowledge: see [GRU 09]) operations were launched with the aim of rationalizing and establishing durable processes for industrial activity, without always requiring the presence of experts. Knowledge-based systems, the associated algorithms and stored data appeared to give companies a certain level of control over employee expertise [GON 86].

However, two significant issues concerning knowledge-based systems emerged during the 1990s. The first, of a technological nature, concerned the rapid evolution of artifacts and hardware, meaning that some of the databases used for knowledge-based systems were becoming obsolete extremely quickly. These systems were based on static data stored in memory, and the workload involved in maintaining and updating these databases was considerable. For example, the data used to calculate piping requirements at *Electricité de France* (EDF) ceased to be relevant with evolutions in material resistance due to the use of new composite materials. The second issue was essentially demographic, concerning the aging population in the western world; this phenomenon presented dangers for businesses in terms of the control of employee expertise, notably with the retirement of senior employees. While knowledge-based systems *may* enable the conservation of knowledge, this is not absolute: once experts leave, companies have very limited means of ensuring that the results provided by the knowledge-based system will be correctly interpreted. Figure 3.5 shows how a simple indicator may or may not have meaning depending on the individual observer. As knowledge-based systems provide no guarantees as to the validity of the meaning given to the information they transmit or of stability between users, they cannot be considered to be KS, as they do not consider knowledge as the result of an individual's interpretation of information.

Figure 3.5. *A warning light on a car dashboard is information which may or may not have meaning for the individual observer*

Tsuchiya [TSU 93], considering knowledge as the result of an individual's interpretation of information, stated that "when information is sense-read through interpretative framework, it becomes knowledge". To fully understand this vision of knowledge, it is useful to consider certain differences between Western and Japanese philosophies, as highlighted by Nonaka and Takeuchi [NON 95].

In Western philosophy, Plato held that ideas were "forms", which might be observed with a pure mind, and which the human spirit aspires to know. For Plato, the physical world is simply a shadow of the idea-world (the cave myth [PLA 78]) and the human being aspires to know these ideas which cannot be perceived, but which can be arrived at through pure reason. Descartes put forward theories of rationalism, where all belief may be doubted, apart from the existence of the questioner: "*cogito, ergo sum*"[1]. For Locke, on the other hand, the human spirit was a blank canvas, learning about things which exist in the world through sensory perception; these things themselves are objective.

Japanese intellectual tradition, on the other hand, does not oppose the "physical world" and the "spirit world", an opposition present in occidental thought for millennia. This tradition centers on three ideas: (1) unity of the human being with nature, (2) unity of body and soul and (3) the unity of self with others. The first idea illustrates the Japanese tendency to explain the link between humans and the natural world through an emotional and sensory experience, rather than through theoretical or metaphysical abstractions. The second idea, the unity of body and soul, contributed to the development of a Zen Buddhist methodology. This methodology included aspects drawn from the Samurai training process, where wisdom was held to

---

1 I think, therefore I am.

be attained through physical training. To be a "man of action" was considered much more important than attaining mastery of philosophy or literature, as wisdom was attained *through action*, and knowledge and action were intrinsically linked. The third and final idea, unity of self and others, arises from the first two principles: the unity of the human being with nature and the unity of body and soul. Although Western philosophy considers human relationships from an atomistic or mechanical perspective, Japanese philosophy considers them to be collective and organic. Western philosophy tends to conceptualize things from an objective perspective, whereas Japanese philosophy does the same thing through interaction, by relating to other individuals or things, so that the three ideas of unity with nature, unity of body and soul and unity of self and others are attained.

Nishida and Jōchi [NIS 70] proposed the concept of *Ba*, developed by Nonaka and Konno [NON 98], who defined it as a "shared space for emerging relationships". This concept was discussed in section 2.3.5.1 and corresponds to a location which synthesizes and gives structure to Japanese intellectual tradition, as presented above. It may be physical (e.g. a meeting room), mental (e.g. shared experiences) or a combination of the two. In this location – a *Ba* – the parties involved can be certain that the three principles of (1) unity of the human being with nature, (2) unity of body and soul and (3) unity of self and others are respected. This creates an environment in which individual and/or collective knowledge can progress. In a *Ba*, human interaction is not limited to an exchange of information, but includes a component which aims to ensure that the desired meaning is also transmitted. The elements of unity, interaction and human presence in a *Ba* ensure that knowledge is shared.

A KS is a system in which information is not considered independently of the meaning it will take on for the recipients. Knowledge is considered to be the result of an individual's interpretation of information, and is the meaning which this information takes for the person in question. This information may be diffused using a variety of media, and is tangible; knowledge, on the other hand, resides in a *Ba* and is intangible [NON 98]. In the same *Ba*, the same information will have the same meaning for any individual. For Nonaka and Konno [NON 98], *Ba* can exist on different levels, and may be connected to form a larger *Ba*, known as a *Basho*. For the authors, grouping *Ba* into a *Basho* amplifies the knowledge creation [NON 98]. A KS may be seen as a *Basho*.

A KS includes individuals and knowledge, i.e. the meaning given to information by these individuals. Outside of a KS, we encounter individuals and information which, detached from its potential meaning, constitutes information as a source of knowledge for those able to interpret it [GRU 09]. For Nonaka and Konno [NON 98], knowledge has no value outside of a *Ba*. Arduin [ARD 14] considered the way in which the same item of information can have different meanings for different individuals.

A KS may also include a DIS, used to store and transmit knowledge which has been rendered explicit and codified.

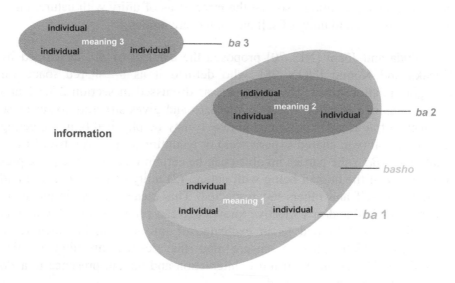

Figure 3.6. *A knowledge system: individuals, information and meanings it takes. For a color version of the figure, see www.iste.co.uk/arduin/information.zip*

Considering the individual as a system component, as a knowledge-holder and information processor, enables the EIKS to be used for knowledge management. The explicit dimension is treated by the individual as an information processor, while the tacit dimension is treated by the individual as a knowledge-holder. These two vectors are necessary and sufficient when considering knowledge, whether explicit or tacit, and form an integral part of EIKS, as they are intrinsically linked to the individual, who is a component in their own right.

3.4. Evolution of an EIKS

IS and KS make use of DIS. DIS constitute the source and support for company decision and management processes, and the framework used to structure the companies in which they are designed and used. These systems have functions which may generate practices and behaviors different from those initially envisaged. Depending on the design of the DIS, underlying models and the platforms used for implementation, this phenomenon can lead to organizational innovations. In this case, value-adding processes may be created and/or modified. This evolution also creates new problems and new requirements; the comprehension and resolution of these problems causes the creation of new knowledge, as well new requirements, leading to new functions being designed.

EIKS management needs to take account of these evolutions, which should be considered from the very beginning of the DIS design process.

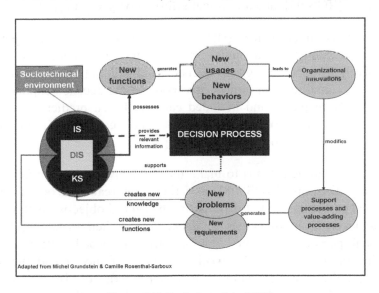

Figure 3.7. *Evolution of the EIKS*

3.5. Representative example of an EIKS

The EIKS has been presented in this book. The EIKS was conceived, deduced, developed and studied based on our research in knowledge management, practical experiences and observation in a company setting.

While the DIS is central to the EIKS, the essential element of the system still lies in the importance of human operators and their knowledge in businesses. The IS itself is not only technical, but also includes a human dimension. This dimension involves considering individuals as system components in their own right, and their knowledge, i.e. the meaning they give to information (sense-giving and sense-reading, see section 3.1.2), should not be neglected. By introducing the EIKS, we aim to replace individuals and their knowledge at the center of business. A representative example of an EIKS will be presented below.

3.5.1. *Presentation of the context*

In 2008, we were able to visit an entertainments business to study its "group decision and negotiation system" for "operational performance management". Interested readers may wish to consult the full study, published in [ROS 08], and additional information given in [IAF 15].

A business intelligence (BI) project at the strategic operational management center of a major theme park in France had evolved progressively to become a group decision and negotiation system (GDNS). This system constituted an improved version of the decision support system (DSS) already in place, and included calendar-based predictions of visitor numbers and origins, along with road traffic and weather conditions, in order to optimize resource allocation across the park.

This type of system tends to make the company in question into a "zero latency organization" [ROS 08], assisting with real-time optimization of operational performance; put differently, the central objective is to minimize the time taken from diagnosis to decision and then to action. From an operational perspective, every day is different. Road traffic may vary depending on the day of the week, the time of month and the season. Weather conditions can affect client behavior in terms of visits to attractions, restaurants and shops. The established system allowed these elements to be monitored, while proposing dynamic resource allocation: increasing or decreasing the number of cash registers at the entrance to the park, the number of mobile salespeople, the number of waiting staff in the restaurants, etc. Over 900 sales points were surveyed every 5 min, and each individual was equipped with a smartphone to enable them to interact with the system.

3.5.2. *EIKS in this context*

EIKS is constructed on top of a socio-technical fabric, i.e. individuals interacting with each other and with machines. This example (illustrated in Figure 3.8) includes:

– an *Information System*, made up of individuals who, while carrying out the processes required for correct operation of the company, process, store and transmit information: these individuals thus act as information processors. An individual on the ground who uses his/her smartphone to indicate that the line at attraction x is longer than y is, for example, a member of the IS, as is a worker who transmits the same information verbally to a colleague;

– a *Knowledge System*, made up of both tacit knowledge, embodied by individuals, and knowledge which has been rendered explicit, formalized and codified using any form of support. The GDNS system at the strategic operational management center, using incoming information from attraction x to infer that the displayed waiting time should be changed, for example, is part of the KS, in the same way as an experienced individual on the ground who would interpret this information in the same way;

– a *Digital Information System*, corresponding to all artifacts designed using ICT, i.e.:

  - the servers and computer terminals at the strategic operational - management center,

  - the "Group Decision and Negotiation System",

  - individual smartphones,

  - cash registers,

  - sensors distributed in and around the park, providing information on:

    - weather,

    - road traffic,

    - visits:

      - to cash registers at the park entrance,

      - to attractions,

      - to shops,

- to restaurants,

- to hotels.

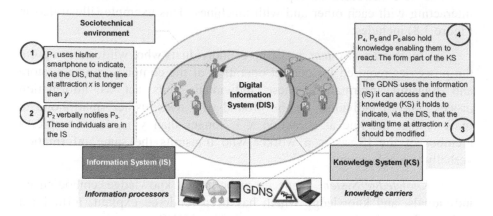

Figure 3.8. *An example of an enterprise's information
and knowledge system (EIKS)*

In this example, the EIKS is made up of three component systems. Within the enterprise, we were able to observe individuals sharing information among themselves, and with the DIS, using ICT-based devices. For example, if the weather conditions deteriorated as the day progressed, the GDNS was able to change individual allocations, moving employees from mobile sales posts to cash registers in the restaurants or shops. This was carried out without face-to-face interaction, simply using the devices included in the DIS. The GDNS thus holds the knowledge required to carry out these actions, which it is able to infer based on incoming information. In addition to technological devices, each individual constitutes a component of the system in their own right, as an information processor and as a knowledge-holder: employees perceive, process, store and transmit information, and hold knowledge which they create based on interpreted information. When this knowledge is rendered explicit, it may then be held by the DIS. In the example shown in Figure 3.8, P_1 could be an information processor as well as a knowledge holder; P_2, acting as a knowledge holder, could also be an information processor. In other words, P_1 and P_2 could be the same person.

3.6. Key points

The key ideas to remember from this chapter are:

– the three postulates: (1) knowledge is not an object, (2) knowledge is linked to action and (3) the company's knowledge includes two main categories of knowledge;

– the EIKS is built on a socio-technical fabric (individuals in interaction with each other, with machines and with the system itself). It includes an IS, a KS and a DIS, constructed using ICT;

– a KS is not a knowledge-based system;

– an individual is a holder of knowledge and a processor of information, and is a component of the EIKS.

Conclusions and Perspectives

The main objective of any company is to produce goods and services. This objective is achieved through the creation of a strategy and through the application of skill sets. To create a strategy, companies implement activities structured around trade processes. These processes require information and knowledge for successful completion.

In any company, all processes are now concerned with information and communications technology (ICT): technology has an impact on professional activities, and these activities have an influence on technology. The two elements are interdependent.

In this book, we have seen the way in which digital information systems (DIS) are now present everywhere, leading to a belief that information systems (IS) are simply numerical and exclusively digital. This view neglects the essential role played by individuals in the system, and, notably, neglects the importance of social capital, as defined by Cohen and Prusak: "Social capital consists of the stock of active connections among people: the trust, mutual understanding, and shared values and behaviors that bind the members of human networks and communities and make cooperative action possible" [COH 01]. Moreover, through the evolution of ICT, digital technology has resulted in shifts in individual habits, with knock-on effects on organization-based professions, organizational processes, research and innovation, direction, communications, client relations, logistics, skills and career management. Digital technology, as defined in Chapter 1, has led to a genuine transformation in organizations, with notable modifications to the relationship between Chief Information Officers (CIOs) and the stakeholders in the IS itself.

ICT appears to evolve independently of organizational activity. It forms part of our everyday and private lives, sometimes to a greater extent than in our professional lives. Each new technological evolution can lead to the creation of new usages. As we have noted, the relationship between technological evolutions and evolutions in their use has changed. Use evolves in the wake of technological evolutions, but precedes organizational changes. Web 2.0 is one example of a technological evolution which has led to changes in use; as a dynamic and multi-device network, Web 2.0 acts as a way of producing interactions. Use has therefore evolved; users no longer simply consult Web pages through a browser, but can themselves create content, whether from home, from work or on the move.

Considering a variety of definitions of the concept of IS, we see that there is never an explicit distinction made between the notions of information and knowledge, and the two terms are often used interchangeably. This is particularly apparent in the context of projects relating to DIS using Web 2.0 and big data applications. The aim of this book is to raise awareness of the risks inherent in this confusion of terms, while presenting the concept of the enterprise's information and knowledge system (EIKS). This concept leads to a clearer definition of the conditions and limits within which knowledge may be seen as an object and treated as information by DIS.

Using three key postulates and theories based on our experience and research work in the field of IS and knowledge management (KM), we have highlighted the nature of this content, which can never be more than information. This information may be processed, stored and transmitted using a DIS. It can also be a source of knowledge, when interpreted by an individual who is able to give it meaning; however, this information is not, in itself, knowledge.

In this context, it is important to rethink our approach to DISs, and to clearly identify their role in businesses. The new role of the DIS has been illustrated through the concept of EIKS. The DIS should be designed in such a way as to integrate users, acting as processors of the information they receive through their own interpretative frameworks, which they then interpret using the tacit knowledge they possess.

The EIKS allows us to establish the correct position of a DIS within an organization, to raise awareness of the place and role of various stakeholders and to highlight the existence of tacit knowledge, carried by individuals. It shows the differences which can exist between individual interpretative frameworks, meaning that the same information may have a different meaning for different people. Moreover, interactions between those involved with the system have an influence on the creation of their own knowledge, their decisions and their actions. It is therefore necessary to be aware of the intentions of these parties, which are not always known and cannot always be managed.

The EIKS is a conceptual representation of an IS, centered on individuals and on digital technology. By modifying the way in which problems are expressed, it opens up new prospects, considerably improving our ability to understand the complex nature of situations and problems. It allows us to identify the most suitable solutions and leads to an increased capacity for innovation. This raises a certain number of questions:

– in terms of governance principles:

- can the EIKS be used as a reference model in order to evaluate the impact of digital technology on the transformation of an organization?

- how can the risks associated with the use and creation of knowledge be integrated, as critical factors, in a digital organization?

– in terms of DIS design:

- can the user be considered as a system component, carrying out information processing and converting this information into knowledge?

– in terms of social responsibility:

- the ubiquity of digital technology raises new issues, and it is important to be aware that people may have different intentions to those we envisage. For example, to what end can this ubiquity be exploited? Do concepts such as big data and cloud computing mean that data can be considered independently of the intentions of individuals?

- does the concept of EIKS help us to define the position of man, as a communicating being, in relation to the possibilities made available by ICT, and to the resulting digital transformations?

Appendix

Seven Golden Rules for Successful Knowledge Management

A.1. Clearly differentiate between the two types of knowledge in the company

Unlike the technological approach, the managerial and socio-technical approach focuses on the nature of knowledge, rather than on its contents. There are two broad categories of knowledge: know-how (explicit knowledge) and skills (tacit knowledge).

The explicit, formalized knowledge of a company constitutes a mass of tangible elements, found in manuals, directions, guides and procedures, analysis and summary documents, databases and computer files, patents, plans, models, algorithms etc.

Skills, which constitute tacit knowledge acquired through practice, are intangible elements such as abilities, knacks, "trade secrets", "routines" (regular and predictable behavior models) – individual and collective unwritten operating practices [NEL 82] – and knowledge of the history and context of decisions.

NOTE.– This approach to knowledge within a company highlights the importance of tacit knowledge. It shows the interest of promoting knowledge exchange and sharing, and of transforming this knowledge into explicit knowledge, enlarging the field of knowledge able to be managed using industrial property rules.

A.2. Increase the focus on individual knowledge

In this context, we have chosen to use the knowledge classification proposed by Michael Polanyi[1]. Based on the fact that "we can know more than we can tell", Polanyi classified human knowledge using two categories: "explicit knowledge refers to knowledge which can be expressed through words, drawings, or other 'articulated' methods, notably metaphors; tacit knowledge is knowledge which is difficult to express, whatever the form of language used" [POL 66]. Thus, it is possible to distinguish between explicit, articulated or formalized individual knowledge, and tacit individual knowledge, which a person may or may not be aware of holding.

NOTE.– Even if individual knowledge acquired by interaction with a group of individuals within a company has a collective dimension, it still remains private in nature, as this individual knowledge is not formalized or disseminated.

A.3. Do not confuse skills with competence

The notions of skills and competence are often confused, and the terms are often considered to be broadly synonymous.

In this context, the notions of competence and skills need to be clearly differentiated. Discussion of the knowledge and skills used and produced within a company does not predetermine the way in which this knowledge will be implemented on a day-to-day basis by individuals in operational situations, subject to technical, economic and psycho-sociological constraints. From this perspective, competence may be understood as "the ability of individuals to implement the physical resources, knowledge and skills making up company knowledge, in addition to their own personal knowledge, in given limited working conditions, including a workstation, a clearly-defined role and a specific mission. Thus, individual competence plays out within the framework of a defined action process. This process, in addition to knowledge and skills, relies on the personal and ethical attitudes of those concerned" [GRU 02].

---

1 Hungarian-born Michael Polanyi was the brother of Karl Polanyi, an economist best known as the author of *The Great Transformation*. Michael Polanyi was a renowned chemist before turning his attention to philosophy at the age of 50 [NON 95].

NOTE.– In a business context, the notion of competence becomes ambiguous, depending on whether it concerns organizational (company) competences, collective (team) competences or individual (professional) competences [DEJ 01].

A.4. Avoid considering knowledge as objects

In order for organizational knowledge, essential for decision and action purposes, to be created, the interpretative frameworks (mental models) of all members of an organization should include at least a minimum level of shared representations, which Tsuchiya refers to as "commensurability". To paraphrase:

> The original source of organizational knowledge is the tacit individual knowledge of members of the organization. However, organizational knowledge is not simply the amalgamation of individual knowledge. Individual knowledge needs to be articulated, shared and legitimized before becoming organizational knowledge. Individual knowledge is shared through dialog. Given that knowledge is essentially tacit, it first needs to be articulated and expressed using language, in the general sense of the term. Next, articulated individual knowledge, which constitutes information for other individuals, needs to be communicated to other members of the organization. It is important to clearly distinguish between information-sharing and knowledge-sharing. Information only becomes knowledge when it is understood via the receiver's interpretation mechanisms, giving it meaning (sense-reading). Any information which is not consistent with this interpretation mechanism is not generally perceived. Thus, the "commensurability" of the interpretation mechanisms of company members is essential to the sharing of individual knowledge [TSU 93].

In summary, knowledge is not an object, but is the result of an interaction between a person and a piece of data.

NOTE.– When a high degree of commensurability is present between interpretative frameworks, knowledge projected through documents or other media may be considered to be, to all intents and purposes, objective. This is notably the case for industrial knowledge, where capitalization for asset creation targets populations of specialists with specific areas of expertise. In these cases, knowledge may be treated as "knowledge objects". This concept is used in solutions such as document management system (DMS) and company and/or project memory bases. However, it is important to remember that whatever is formalized, in whatever form, can never be more than information, which takes on meaning only for those in possession of shared interpretation mechanism. Thus, as the active population evolves, interpretation mechanisms evolve, and this can raise difficulties with regard to access and interpretation, creating a risk of erroneous use of these "knowledge objects".

A.5. Clearly differentiate between the three types of information

Global access to information, via a "company portal", raises issues concerning the nature of information to which an actor/decision maker should have access. This problem, raised in research report #11 [GRU 05], leads us to distinguish between three different types of information: main-stream information, making up the information flow and concerning the state of production and operating processes in the company; shared information, treated using information and communication technology (ICT); and information as a source of knowledge, notably resulting from a knowledge engineering approach proposing techniques and tools for acquiring and representing knowledge.

NOTE.– In this context, it is important to think about the best technological and organizational approach to designing a digital information system, with the intention of allowing actors to obtain main-stream information, share tacit knowledge and access relevant information as a source of knowledge from their own workstation. This information is needed in order to solve problems, make decisions, complete activities and capitalize on the knowledge produced in the course of these activities.

A.6. Correctly position the concept of knowledge management

We believe that the concept of knowledge management (KM) should be positioned in relation to the knowledge capitalization issue in companies. This issue consists of a set of recurring problems which the company has always had to deal with, and is characterized by five elements and their interactions. Each of these elements is the object of subprocesses which aim to provide a solution to all of the problems concerned. These problems, described in Research Report #11 [GRU 05], are integrated into the "Model for General Knowledge Management within the Enterprise" (MGKME).

NOTE.– The managerial approach to KM concerns all actions which aim to respond to the knowledge capitalization problem as a whole. It results in "processes intended to manage the deployment of skills and to increase the use and creation of knowledge, with two key aims: an asset-based aim, linked to knowledge, and a sustainable development aim, linked to skills and to knowledge" [BOU 03]. This approach focuses on two interlinked aims, one of asset creation and one of sustainable development. It forms part of the "Model for General Knowledge Management within the Enterprise" (MGKME).

A.7. Include all four dimensions of KM

Our approach to KM includes four basic dimensions, each of which is essential to the study and establishment of a KM project in a company.

A.7.1. *The economic and strategic dimension*

This dimension concerns the competitive environment engendered by globalization and economic liberalization, which has demonstrated the power of organizational networks, shown the necessity of sustainable development criteria and lead to an increased awareness of the value of immaterial capital.

A.7.2. *The organizational dimension*

This dimension concerns the company, its values, structure, the way it is directed and operates, its economic and financial criteria, key skills, value-adding processes, and knowledge capitalization activities and processes to promote, organize and develop.

A.7.3. *The sociocultural dimension*

This dimension concerns the behavior of groups and individuals, as actors in a company's knowledge capitalization process: their needs, abilities, areas of autonomy, responsibilities, competence, the way in which they are paid, professional culture, ethics and values, and ability to establish "relationships of good understanding"[2].

A.7.4. *The technological dimension*

This dimension concerns all skills, techniques, methods and tools which provide the necessary support for the implementation of activities and the successful completion of knowledge capitalization processes.

NOTE.– An organization must evolve on its own, increasing diversity by creating new thought and behavioral mechanisms. In this context, defining KM as "management of activities and processes destined to increase the use and creation of knowledge within businesses", KM must be perceived through a prism made up of four complementary dimensions, their connections and interactions: the economic and strategic dimension, the organizational dimension, the sociocultural dimension and the technological dimension.

---

2 Many authors consider that the conditions for knowledge-sharing rely on "trust relationships" between actors. Thinking in terms of individual knowledge, the intentions and emotional aspect of humans become central to the trust relationship. Thus, these factors should not be left out when analyzing organizational conditions intended to promote knowledge-sharing. This appears somewhat optimistic in industrial and commercial organizations motivated by power and money. It is, therefore, preferable to consider organizational conditions which promote "relationships of good understanding" as a basis for trust, i.e. relationships founded on four criteria: respect of self and others, the complementarity of skills, the reciprocal nature of exchange and transparency in decisions concerning the object of shared working processes.

Bibliography

[ALA 01] ALAVI M., LEIDNER D.E., "Knowledge management and knowledge management systems: conceptual foundations and research issue", *MIS Quarterly*, vol. 25, no. 1, pp. 107–136, March 2001.

[ALT 00] ALTER N., *L'innovation ordinaire*, Presses Universitaires de France, Paris, France, 2000.

[ARD 13a] ARDUIN P.-E., Vers une métrique de la commensurabilité des schémas d'interprétation, PhD Thesis, Paris-Dauphine University, Paris, France, 26 September 2013.

[ARD 13b] ARDUIN P.-E., GRUNDSTEIN M., ROSENTHAL-SABROUX C., "From knowledge sharing to collaborative decision making", *International Journal of Information and Decision Sciences*, vol. 5, no. 3, pp. 295–311, 2013.

[ARD 14] ARDUIN P.-E., "On the use of cognitive maps to identify meaning variance", *Lecture Notes in Business Information Processing*, Springer, vol. 180, pp. 73–80, 2014.

[ARG 96] ARGYRIS C., SCHÖN D.A., *Organizational Learning II: Theory, Method, and Practice*, Addison-Wesley Publishing Company, Readings, MA, 1996.

[ARG 03] ARGYRIS C., *Savoir pour Agir*, Dunod, Paris, 2003.

[BAL 02] BALMISSE G., *Gestion des connaissances. Outils et applications du Knowledge Management*, Vuibert, Paris, 2002.

[BOU 03] BOUCHER X., HARZALLAH M., VERNADAT F., "Articulation entre compétences et connaissances en génie industriel", *Cinquième Congrès International de Génie Industriel, Le Génie industriel et les nouveaux défis mondiaux*, Quebec, Canada, October 2003.

[CHA 94] CHAMBAT P., "Usages des technologies de l'information et de la communication (TIC): évolution des problématiques", *TIC et Sociétés*, vol. 6, no. 3, pp. 249–270, 1994.

[CHA 00] CHARLET J., ZACKLAD M., KASSEL G. *et al.*, *Ingénierie des connaissances. Evolutions récentes et nouveaux efies*, Editions Eyrolles et France Télécom-CNET, Paris, France, 2000.

[CHU 71] CHURCHMAN C.W., *The Design of Inquiring Systems*, Basic Books, New York, 1971.

[CHU 04] CHUA B.B., BRENNAN J., "Enhancing collaborative knowledge management systems design", in REMENYI D. (ed.), *5th European Conference on Knowledge Management*, Academic Conferences Limited, Reading, UK, pp. 171–178, 2004.

[CIG 00] CIGREF, Gérer les connaissances. Défi, enjeux et conduite de projet, Report no. ATTJ8KE4. CIGREF, Club informatique des grandes entreprises françaises, Paris, available at http://www.cigref.fr, pp. 15–17, 2000.

[COA 02] COAKES E., "Knowledge management: a sociotechnical perspective", in COKES E., WILLIS D., CLARKE S. (eds), *Knowledge Management in the Sociotechnical World*, Springer-Verlag, London, pp. 4–14, 2002.

[COB 05] COBIT®, "Gouvernance, Contrôle et Audit de l'Information et des Technologies Associées (Control Objectives for Information and Related Technology)", *Information Systems Audit and Control*, 3rd ed., IT Governance Institute, Rolling Meadows, IL, 2005.

[COH 01] COHEN D., PRUSAK L., *In Good Company: How Social Capital Makes Organizations Work*, Harvard Business School Publishing, Boston, MA, 2001.

[COM 90] COMMISSION CENTRALE DES MARCHÉS (CCM), Conduite de projet informatique, Editions d'Organisation, 1990.

[COU 93] COURBON J.C., *Systèmes d'information: structuration, modélisation et communication*, Inter Editions, 1993.

[DAV 98] DAVENPORT T., PRUSAK L., *Working Knowledge: How Organizations Manage What They Know*, Harvard University Press, 1998.

[DAV 00] DAVID A., "Logique, épistémologie et méthodologie en sciences de gestion: trois hypothèses revisitées", in DAVID A., HATCHUEL A., LAUFER R. (eds), *Les nouvelles fondations des sciences de gestion. Elément d'épistémologie de la recherche en management*, Vuibert, Paris, France, pp. 83–109, 2000.

[DEJ 01] DEJOUX C., *Les compétences au cœur de l'entreprise*, Editions d'Organisation, 2001.

[DEM 92] DEMING W.E., *Out of the Crisis*, MIT Press, MA, 1992.

[DIN 99] DINUCCI D., "Fragmented future", *Print*, vol. 53, no. 4, p. 32, 1999.

[DOR 99] DORTIER J.-F., RUANO-BORBALAN J.-C., "Les théories de l'organisation: un continent éclaté?", in CABIN P. (ed.), *Les organisations. Etat des savoirs*, Sciences Humaines Editions, Auxerre, France, pp. 27–38, 1999.

[DRU 93] DRUCKER P., *Au-delà du Capitalisme, La métamorphose de cette fin de siècle*, Dunod, Paris, France, 1993.

[EDV 97] EDVINSSON L., MALONE M., *Intellectual Capital, Realizing Your Company's True Value by Finding Its Hidden Brainpower*, Harper Collins Publishers, Inc., New York, 1997.

[ERM 94] ERMES-GROUPE ESCP, *Systèmes D'Information: La perspective du management*, Ed. Masson, 1994.

[FEE 04] FEENBERG A., *Repenser la technique. Vers une technologie démocratique*, La Découverte, Paris, 2004.

[FER 68] TERRY H., *L'obélisque de Louxor*, Bibliothèque Nationale de France, 1868.

[GAN 93] GANASCIA J.G., *L'Intelligence artificielle*, Dominos Flammarion, 1993.

[GON 86] GONDRAN M., *Introduction aux systèmes experts*, Eyrolles, 1986.

[GRU 88] GRUNDSTEIN M., DE BONNIÈRES P., PARA S., *Les systèmes à base de connaissances. Systèmes experts pour l'entreprise*, Afnor Gestion, Paris, 1988.

[GRU 92] GRUNDSTEIN M., "Knowledge engineering within the company: an approach to constructing and capitalizing the knowledge assets of the company", *Third Annual Symposium of the International Association of Knowledge Engineers*, Washington DC, November 16–19, 1992.

[GRU 95] GRUNDSTEIN M., "La Capitalisation des Connaissances de l'Entreprise, Système de production des connaissances", *Actes du Colloque L'Entreprise Apprenante et les sciences de la complexité*, University of Provence, Aix-en-Provence, 22–24 May 1995.

[GRU 98] GRUNDSTEIN M., Le management des connaissances de l'entreprise: Research report no. 019806, MG Conseil, Paris, June 1998.

[GRU 00] GRUNDSTEIN M., "From capitalizing on company's knowledge to knowledge management", in MOREY D., MAYBURY M., THURAISINGHAM B. (eds), *Knowledge Management: Classic and Contemporary Works*, MIT Press, Cambridge, MA, 2000.

[GRU 01] GRUNDSTEIN M., ROSENTHAL-SABROUX C., "Vers un système d'information source de connaissance", in CAUVET C., ROSENTHAL-SABROUX C. (eds), *Ingénierie des Systèmes d'Information*, Hermes Science-Lavoisier, Paris, 2001.

[GRU 02] GRUNDSTEIN M., "De la capitalisation des connaissances au renforcement des compétences dans l'entreprise étendue", *1er Colloque du groupe de travail Gestion des Compétences et des Connaissances en Génie Industriel*, Nantes, 12–13 December 2002.

[GRU 03] GRUNDSTEIN M., ROSENTHAL-SABROUX C., "Three types of data for extended company's employees: a knowledge management viewpoint", in KHOSROW-POUR M. (ed.), *Information Technology and Organizations: Trends, Issues, Challenges and Solutions*, Idea Group Publishing, Hershey, PA, 2003.

[GRU 04] GRUNDSTEIN M., ROSENTHAL-SABROUX C., "GAMETH®, a decision support approach to identify and locate potential crucial knowledge", in REMENYI D. (ed.), *Proceedings of the 5th European Conference on Knowledge Management*, Academic Conferences Limited, Reading, UK, pp. 391–402, 2004.

[GRU 05] GRUNDSTEIN M., Vers un Modèle Général de Knowledge Management pour l'Entreprise (MGKME), Research report no. 11, available at http://www.mgconseil.fr, 25 January 2005.

[GRU 08] GRUNDSTEIN M., ROSENTHAL-SABROUX C., "A global vision of inofrmation management", *Proceedings of MoDiSE-EUS*, pp. 55–66, 2008.

[GRU 09] GRUNDSTEIN M., ROSENTHAL-SABROUX C., "Vers une approche du système d'information et de connaissance transposée de l'approche du knowledge management dans l'entreprise étendue", in ROSENTHAL-SABROUX C., CARVALHO A., *Management et gouvernance des SI*, Hermes Science-Lavoisier, Paris, 2009.

[GRU 12] GRUNDSTEIN M., "Three postulates that change knowledge management paradigm", in HOU H.T., *New Research on Knowledge Management Models and Methods*, In Tech, 2012.

[GUI 93] GUILLAUME M., "Le génie des réseaux et de la communication", in SFEZ L. (ed.), *Dictionnaire de la communication*, vol. 1, Presses Universitaires de France, Paris, pp. 296–305, 1993.

[HAE 00] HAECKEL S., "Managing Knowledge in Adaptive Enterprises", in DESPRES C., CHAUVEL D. (eds), *Knowledge Horizon*, Butterworth-Heinemann, vol. 14, pp. 287–305, 2000.

[HAL 97] HALL B.P., *Understanding Values as a Foundation to Knowledge Intensive Business*, San Francisco, 20–21 February 1997.

[HOR 09] HORNUNG B.R., "Constructing sociology from first order cybernetics: Basic concepts for a sociocybernetic analysis of information society", *Proceedings of the 4th Conference of Sociocybernetics*, Corfu, Greece, 2009.

[IAF 15] IAFRATE F., *From Big Data to Smart Data*, ISTE Ltd, London and John Wiley & Sons, New York, 2015.

[IMK 90] IMKA, *IMKA Technology Technical Summary*, July 30, 1990.

[INM 93] INMON W.H., *Le développement des applications client/serveur*, Ed. Masson, 1993.

[ISO 91] ISO/IEC 9126, Information technology – software product evaluation – quality characteristics and guidelines for their use, International Standard, 1991.

[JAC 98] JACKSON P., *Introduction to Expert Systems*, Addison-Wesley, 1998.

[JEN 05] JENNEX M.E., ADDO T.B.A., "Issues in knowledge management strategy", in KHOSROW-POUR M. (ed.), *Managing Modern Organization with Information Technology*, Idea Group Publishing, Hershey, PA, 2005.

[JON 11] JONES N.A., ROSS H., LYNAM T. *et al.*, "Mental models: An interdisciplinary synthesis of theory and methods", *Ecology and Society*, vol. 16, no. 1, 2011.

[KAS 95] KASSEL G., Contribution à la représentation des connaissances pour les systèmes experts de 2nde génération: le projet AIDE, Thesis, University of Technology of Compiègne, 1995.

[KET 98] KETTANI N., MIGNET D., PARÉ P., *De MERISE à UML*, Eyrolles, 1998.

[LEG 74] LE GOFF J., "Les mentalités – une histoire ambiguë", in LE GOFF J., NORA P. (eds), *Faire de l'histoire – Nouveaux problèmes*, Gallimard, Paris, vol. 3, 1974.

[LEM 74] LE MOIGNE J.L., *Les systèmes d'information dans les organisations*, Presses Universitaires de France, Paris, 1974.

[LEM 77] LE MOIGNE J.L., *Théorie du système général, théorie de la modélisation*, Presses Universitaires de France, Paris, 1977.

[LEM 90] LE MOIGNE J.L., *La modélisation des systèmes complexes*, Dunod, 1990.

[LEM 91] LE MOIGNE J.L., "La conception des systèmes d'information organisationnels: de l'ingénierie informatique à l'ingénierie des systèmes", *Autour et a L'entour de MERISE*, AFCET Sophia Antipolis, April 1991.

[LEO 95] LEONARD-BARTON D., *Wellsprings of Knowledge: Building and Sustaining the Sources of Innovation*, Harvard Business School Press, 1995.

[LEP 95] LE PETIT ROBERT, *Dictionnaire alphabétique et analogique de la langue française*, Dictionnaires Le Robert/VUEF, Paris, 1995.

[LEQ 99] LEQUEUX J.-L., *Manager avec les ERP*, Editions d'Organisation, 1999.

[MCG 71] MC GREGOR D., *La dimension humaine de l'entreprise*, Gauthier-Villars Editeur, Paris, 1971.

[MÉL 79] MÉLÈSE J., *Approches systémique des organisations*, Hommes et Techniques, Paris, 1979.

[MÉN 10] MÉNARD B., *L'entreprise numérique*, Nuvis, 2010.

[MID 77] MIDLER C., *L'auto qui n'existait pas*, InterEditions, Paris, 1993.

[MOR 77] MORIN E., *La méthode*, Seuil, Paris, 1977.

[NAN 92] NANCI D., ESPINASSE B., COHEN B., *Ingénierie des systèmes d'information avec Merise: Vers une deuxième génération*, Sybex, 1992.

[NEL 82] NELSON R.R., WINTER S.G., *An Evolutionary Theory of Economic Change*, Harvard University Press, Cambridge, MA, 1982.

[NIS 70] NISHIDA K., JÔCHI D., Fundamental Problems of Philosophy: The World of Action and the Dialectical World, Thesis, Sophia University, 1970.

[NON 95] NONAKA I., TAKEUCHI H., *The Knowledge Creating Company*, Oxford University Press, New York, 1995.

[NON 98] NONAKA I., KONNO N., "The concept of 'Ba': building a foundation for knowledge creation", *California Management Review*, vol. 40, no. 3, pp. 40–54, Spring 1998.

[NON 00] NONAKA I., TOYAMA R., KONNO N., "SECI, Ba and leadership: a unified model of dynamic knowledge creation", *Long Range Planning*, vol. 33, pp. 5–34, 2000.

[O'RE   05]   O'REILLY   T.,   What   is   Web   2.0?,   available   at
http://www.oreilly.com/pub/a/oreilly/tim/news/2005/09/30/what-is-web-20.html,
2005.

[OSB 64] OSBORN A.F., *L'imagination constructive. Créativité et brainstorming*,
Dunod, Paris, 1964.

[PAC 01] PACHULSKI A., Le repérage des connaissances cruciales pour l'entreprise:
concepts, méthode et outils, PhD Thesis, Paris-Dauphine University, France,
19 December 2001.

[PIE 96] PIERRAT C., MARTORY B., *La gestion de l'immatériel*, Nathan, 1996.

[PLA 78] PLATO, *The Republic*, Edition d'Henri Estienne, 1578.

[PLA 00] PLANE J.-M., *Théorie des organisations*, Dunod, Paris, 2000.

[POL 58] POLANYI M., *Personal Knowledge: Towards a Post-Critical Philosophy*,
Routledge, London, 1958.

[POL 66] POLANYI M., *The Tacit Dimension*, Routledge & Kegan Paul Ltd, London,
1966.

[POL   67]   POLANYI   M.,   "Sense-giving   and   sense-reading",   *Philosophy:
Journal of the Royal Institute of Philosophy*, vol. 42, no. 162, pp. 301–323,
1967.

[POR 85] PORTER M.E., *Competitive Advantage: Creating and Sustaining Superior
Performance*, Free Press, New York, 1985.

[PRA 97] PRAX J.-Y., *Manager la connaissance dans l'entreprise*, INSEP Éditions,
1997.

[REG 07] REGAN E.A., "Knowledge management: evolving concept and practice",
The International Journal of Knowledge, Culture and Change Management,
vol. 6, no. 9, pp. 11–24, 2007.

[REI 90] REIX R., *Informatique appliquée à la gestion*, Foucher, 1990.

[RIC 87] RICH E., *Intelligence artificielle*, Masson, 1987.

[ROH 14] ROHMER J., *Des tabulatrices aux tablettes*, Nuvis, 2014.

[ROS 96] ROSENTHAL-SABROUX C., Contribution méthodologique à la conception
de   systèmes   d'information   coopératifs: prise   en   compte   de   la
coopération homme/machine, Thesis, Paris-Dauphine University, Paris, France,
1996.

[ROS 08] ROSENTHAL-SABROUX C., GRUNDSTEIN M., IAFRATE F., "A knowledge worker desktop model (KWDM) applied to decision support system", *Encyclopedia of Decision Making and Decision Support Technologies*, IGI Global, vol. 2, 2008.

[SAA 05] SAAD I., Une contribution méthodologique pour l'aide à l'identification et l'évaluation des connaissances nécessitant une opération de capitalisation, PhD Thesis, Paris-Dauphine University, Paris, France, 22 June 2005.

[SHI 95] SHIMIZU H., "Ba principle: new logic for the real-time emergence of information", *Holonics*, vol. 5, no. 1, pp. 67–79, 1995.

[SHO 76] SHORTLIFFE E.H., *Computer-Based Medical Consultations: MYCIN*, Elsevier, New York, 1976.

[STE 91] STEWART K., "On the politics of cultural theory: a case for contaminated cultural critique", *Social Research*, vol. 58, no. 2, pp. 395–412, 1991.

[STE 01] STEWART A., The conversing company, its culture, power and potential, available at http://www.knowledgeboard.com/download/3343/conversing-company.pdf, 2001.

[TON 04] TONCHIA S., "Knowledge management in enterprise networks", in TONCHIA S., TRAMONTANO A. (eds), *Process Management for the Extended Enterprise*, Springer-Verlag, Berlin-Heidelberg, pp. 47–67, 2004.

[TRA 13] TRAN S., DAVID A., MONOMAKHOFF N. *et al.* (eds), *L'impact du web 2.0 sur les organisations*, Springer, Paris, 2013.

[TSU 93] TSUCHIYA S., "Improving knowledge creation ability through organizational learning", *International Symposium on the Management of Industrial and Corporate Knowledge, ISMICK'93 Proceedings*, UTC-IIIA, Compiègne, France, 1993.

[WEN 00] WENSLEY A.K.P., VERWIJK-O'SULLIVAN A., "Tools for knowledge management", in DESPRES C., CHAUVEL D. (eds), *Knowledge Horizon: The Present and the Promise of Knowledge Management*, Butterworth-Heinemann, Woburn, MA, pp. 113–130, 2000.

[WII 04] WIIG K., *People-focused Knowledge Management: How Effective Decision Making Leads to Corporate Success*, Elsevier Butterworth-Heinemann, Burlington, MA, 2004.

Index

Index

Other titles from

in

Information Systems, Web and Pervasive Computing

2015

IAFRATE Fernando
From Big Data to Smart Data

LAURENT Maryline, BOUZEFRANE Samia
Digital Identity Management

POMEROL Jean-Charles, EPELBOIN Yves, THOURY Claire
MOOCs

2014

DINET Jérôme
Information Retrieval in Digital Environments

DUBÉ Jean, LEGROS Diègo
Spatial Econometrics Using Microdata

HÉNO Raphaële, CHANDELIER Laure
3D Modeling of Buildings: Outstanding Sites

KEMBELLEC Gérald, CHARTRON Ghislaine, SALEH Imad
Recommender Systems

DAUPHINÉ André
Fractal Geography

LEMBERGER Pirmin, MOREL Mederic
Managing Complexity of Information Systems

STOCKINGER Peter
Introduction to Audiovisual Archives

STOCKINGER Peter
Digital Audiovisual Archives

VENTRE Daniel
Cyberwar and Information Warfare

2010

BONNET Pierre
Enterprise Data Governance

BRUNET Roger
Sustainable Geography

CARREGA Pierre
Geographical Information and Climatology

CAUVIN Colette, ESCOBAR Francisco, SERRADJ Aziz
Thematic Cartography – 3-volume series
Thematic Cartography and Transformations – volume 1
Cartography and the Impact of the Quantitative Revolution – volume 2
New Approaches in Thematic Cartography – volume 3

LANGLOIS Patrice
Simulation of Complex Systems in GIS

MATHIS Philippe
Graphs and Networks – 2nd edition

THERIAULT Marius, DES ROSIERS François
Modeling Urban Dynamics

2009

BONNET Pierre, DETAVERNIER Jean-Michel, VAUQUIER Dominique
Sustainable IT Architecture: the Progressive Way of Overhauling Information Systems with SOA

PAPY Fabrice
Information Science

RIVARD François, ABOU HARB Georges, MERET Philippe
The Transverse Information System

ROCHE Stéphane, CARON Claude
Organizational Facets of GIS

VENTRE Daniel
Information Warfare

2008

BRUGNOT Gérard
Spatial Management of Risks

FINKE Gerd
Operations Research and Networks

GUERMOND Yves
Modeling Process in Geography

KANEVSKI Michael
Advanced Mapping of Environmental Data

MANOUVRIER Bernard, LAURENT Ménard
Application Integration: EAI, B2B, BPM and SOA

PAPY Fabrice
Digital Libraries

2007

DOBESCH Hartwig, DUMOLARD Pierre, DYRAS Izabela
Spatial Interpolation for Climate Data

SANDERS Lena
Models in Spatial Analysis

2006

CLIQUET Gérard
Geomarketing

CORNIOU Jean-Pierre
Looking Back and Going Forward in IT

DEVILLERS Rodolphe, JEANSOULIN Robert
Fundamentals of Spatial Data Quality

Printed and bound by CPI Group (UK) Ltd, Croydon, CR0 4YY

27/10/2024

14580729-0001